PLAYING THE GAME

PLAYING THE GAME

Selected Poems of Henry Newbolt

EDITED BY
JOHN HOWLETT

LIVERPOOL UNIVERSITY PRESS

First published 2023 by
Liverpool University Press
4 Cambridge Street
Liverpool
L69 7ZU

Introduction and editorial apparatus © John Howlett
Poems by Henry Newbolt are out of copyright.

John Howlett has asserted the right to be identified as the editor of this book in accordance with the Copyright, Designs and Patents Act 1988.

All rights reserved. No part of this book may be reproduced, stored in a retrieval system, or transmitted, in any form or by any means, electronic, mechanical, photocopying, recording, or otherwise, without the prior written permission of the publisher.

British Library Cataloguing-in-Publication data
A British Library CIP record is available

ISBN 978-1-78976-136-8

Typeset by Carnegie Book Production, Lancaster
Printed and bound by CPI Group (UK) Ltd, Croydon CR0 4YY

Contents

Introduction   1

The Poems   57
from Admirals All and Other Verses, 1897   57
Admirals All   57
San Stefano   59
Drake's Drum   60
Hawke   61
The Fighting Téméraire   62
Vitaï Lampada   63
He Fell Among Thieves   64
Ionicus   65
Minora Sidera   66

from The Island Race, 1898   68
The Vigil   68
Admiral Death   69

Messmates	70
The Death of Admiral Blake	70
The Non-Combatant	72
Clifton Chapel	72
The Echo	73
Fidele's Grassy Tomb	74
Imogen	76
Nel Mozzo del Cammín	77
The Invasion	77
Ireland, Ireland	78
Moonset	78
from The Sailing of the Long-Ships and Other Poems, 1902	80
The Sailing of the Long-Ships	80
Waggon Hill	81
The Volunteer	81
The Schoolfellow	82
The Only Son	82
The School at War	83
By the Hearth-Stone	84
Commemoration	84
The Nile	85
Outward Bound	86
From Generation to Generation	87
When I Remember	87

CONTENTS

The Viking's Song	88
Yattendon	88
A Sower	89
Northumberland	89
from Songs of Memory and Hope, 1909	91
Sacrementum Supremum	91
Devon	91
The Mossrose	92
Ave, Soror	92
To a River in the South	93
The Presentation	93
Amore Altiero	94
Against Oblivion	95
The Inheritance	95
The Pedlar's Song	96
An Essay on Criticism	97
Le Byron de Nos Jours; or, The English Bar and Cross Reviewers	100
from Poems: New and Old, 1912	103
April on Waggon Hill	103
Songs of the Fleet:	104
I. Sailing at Dawn	104
II. The Song of the Sou' Wester	104
III. The Middle Watch	106

IV. The Little Admiral	106
V. The Song of the Guns at Sea	107
VI. Farewell	108
Rilloby-Rill	109
from St. George's Day and Other Poems, 1918	111
The War Films	111
St. George's Day	111
Hic Jacet	112
The King's Highway	113
A Chanty of the Emden	114
The Toy Band	116
A Letter from the Front	117
from A Perpetual Memory and Other Poems, 1939	118
The Great Memory	118
March 5, 1921	119
The Linnet's Nest	119
The Nightjar	120
The Star in the West	121
A Perpetual Memory	121
To Christopher	121
A Letter to R.B. after a Visit	122
Cricket	123
Epitaph on a Public Man	123

CONTENTS

The Old to the Young — 123
Poet's Epitaph — 124

Appendix A – Notes — 125
Appendix B – Goodchild's Garland: Diversions and
    Perversions, 1909 — 139
Index — 151

Introduction

Sir Henry Newbolt (1862–1938) wrote some of the best-known poems in the history of English verse and was, in his time, among the most acclaimed and successful of authors, rivalling even Kipling for popularity and reputation. Chunks of 'Drake's Drum' and 'Vitaï Lampada' in particular were able to be recalled verbatim by almost every schoolchild born in the first three decades of the twentieth century. Likewise, the refrain of '"Play up! play up! and play the game!"' ('Vitaï Lampada', line 8) remains, to this day, one of the most widely quoted lines in the entire canon. Newbolt's books of verse sold in numbers rarely equalled before or since and he was widely anthologized. Any new poems, which often appeared in the popular press prior to being collected in book form, were eagerly awaited and became events. Without any suggestion of exaggeration or self-aggrandizement, Newbolt in later life could reflect how 'The time even came when Ministers quoted me in the House, and Bishops recited me in sermons at St Paul's before the King and Queen' (Newbolt, 1932: 203). Nor was Newbolt's literary achievement confined solely to poetry; he was also variously a novelist, historian, editor, critic, essayist, educator, and government panjandrum and, in so being, can rightly be considered as one of the last genuine Men of Letters whose friendships spanned the gamut of public life, from the arts to politics. As his son-in-law rightly put it, 'He was an Elizabethan in this age of specialists' (Furse, 1939: xvi).

Yet for one so esteemed and decorated, Newbolt's critical reputation has in more recent times gone into a steep decline and his name has become the subject of derision. Much of this was fuelled by the manner in which he became seen as a mouthpiece for the worst traits of his age and, as such, he has been decried as an anachronism – a Victorian inhabiting an Edwardian era. This free fall started even in his own lifetime: 'Newbolt, with an irritating monotony of metre, and a great appearance of nobility, celebrated the worst side of Imperialism' (Batho and Dobrée, 1938: 72). Such views have persisted and have served to pigeon-hole Newbolt as an apologist both for empire (worse still, the *British Empire*) but also excessive forms of nationalist zeal. As recently as 2013 and the discovery of a bumptious piece of juvenilia by Winston Churchill, it was inevitably the 'schoolboy jingoism' (Amelia Hill in *The Guardian*, 6 February 2013) of Newbolt that was used as a point of comparison. A similar notion was put forward by the philosopher Roger Scruton, who identified a subtle strain of anti-Englishness amongst those who could write so lazily of Newbolt's 'inglorious odes' (Scruton, 2006: 245). More tritely, Newbolt's name and perennially famous line are still wheeled out every so often by the more partisan quarters of the press seeking to define what they perceive to be the very best of British virtues, even in the face of (in this case predictable cricketing) defeat: 'Well, I blame Sir Henry Newbolt, the Edwardian poet, and his stirring Vita [sic] Lampada. He was the one who created the idea that it is not the winning that counts, it is the taking part' (Philip Knightley in *The Daily Mail*, 19 December 2006). That this was very much *not* what the poem was about seems, in this case, hardly to matter. These concerns were best encapsulated by Patrick Howarth who created a trope out of the type of character we are supposed to imagine both read and inhabited Newbolt's poetry. Such an endangered species – neatly christened *homo newboltiensis* – was an ideal of his age: 'Imbued with a strong sense of institutional loyalty, upper middle class by background, conformist in belief, dedicated to a concept, not simply of "my country right or wrong," but of a nation enjoying a natural moral prerogative, accepting ungrudgingly the demands of service and duty, inclined to treat women either as companions or as unmentionable' (Howarth, 1973: 13–14).

That Newbolt himself embodied certain aspects of his time is undeniable. Which poet, after all, does not? However, to judge the views he may have held according to contemporary standards is absurdly a-historical, although these days such a fallacy is hardly uncommon, whilst the origins of those derisory critical readings are similarly wholly predictable and the refrains equally tiresome. Crucially, such broad generalizations belie the complexities of the man himself. Indeed, far from being blimpish, Newbolt was a lifelong Liberal who supported a range of more progressive political causes including Irish Home Rule – see for instance the poem 'Ireland, Ireland'. He subsequently displayed his political colours when editor of *The Monthly Review* in which he penned a number of important, and occasionally provocative, essays and articles. Such activity was much to the chagrin of the magazine's Tory benefactor John Murray who was to dismiss him over ideological differences. Furthermore, Newbolt also took a keen interest in radical education, attending various conferences and chairing the committee responsible for the government report bearing his name which sought to re-connect children to the joy of literature. Nor was he the fusty, buttoned up late Victorian we would like to imagine with Susan Chitty's recent (1997) biography implicating him in a long-standing *ménage à trois* with his wife's bisexual cousin.

As with the life, so with the art. That Newbolt could on occasion allow his political message, often one designed for popular consumption, to tramp down on poetic sentiment would be a fair observation. It might also be claimed with some justification that his lifelong obsession with public schools was a living manifestation of Cyril Connolly's (1938) 'Theory of Permanent Adolescence'; in Newbolt's case this was to be found in his devotion to forms of chivalry and fraternal bonds which were a grown-up version of the friendships and house loyalties found amongst schoolboys. However, although such criticisms are valid, we should not in the first instance automatically be suspicious of poets who achieve great popularity – after all, many of Newbolt's hearty and rallying ballads invoking the heroic figures and deeds of England's past frequently display a lithe craftsmanship and stand as masterpieces of their kind. Nor is Newbolt's poetry one dimensional; following the early rousing works came a middle-period shift toward an 'elegiac wistfulness' (Bright, 1990: 157–158) in which straightforward forms of patriotism gave way to more subtle types of commemoration which often have as their theme the transient nature of life and action. Equally as striking is the period from 1918 onwards in which, despite long poetic silences, we still find occasional pieces that are yet more contemplative and lyrical. These in their way reflected the post-war 'return to order' which saw Newbolt reconnecting to the rural landscapes of his beloved Wiltshire and Somerset where he spent increasing amounts of time. Although in the main his poetry never strayed too far from its traditional concerns, Newbolt was surprisingly diverse in his wider literary tastes; his edited anthology *New Paths on Helicon* (1927) for instance included perceptive commentaries on modernists like Ezra Pound, Roy Campbell, and Edith Sitwell and he was a constant agitator for the printing and dissemination of contemporary writing.

To say, however, that in being too often discredited and poorly appraised Newbolt has been correspondingly allowed to fade into obscurity would be inaccurate. The 1990s saw a small resurgence of academic interest which included not just a full-length biography (the aforementioned work by Susan Chitty) but also a magisterial critical study by his great-granddaughter (Vanessa Furse Jackson) as well as Michael Bright's shorter essay which helpfully contained a complete bibliography of Newbolt's copious writings. More widely, Newbolt is also today remembered by a plaque near his birthplace in Bilston, which stands a few streets away from a Wetherspoons chain pub named in his honour! Even so, a proper reissuing of his poems has until now proven elusive with only Patric Dickinson's (1981) and John Betjeman's (1940) selections – made over forty and eighty years ago respectively and both long out of print – being the only previous editions. Even these, though, were to some extent unsatisfactory due to the way in which the authors sought to compartmentalize Newbolt's poems into particular types. Dickinson, for instance, made a point of distinguishing between the lyrics and ballads, a distinction made with even more vigour in Betjeman's earlier edition in which he divided Newbolt's poems into '(1) nautical and patriotic, (2) nostalgic, with vivid pictures of school, education, and English scenery, and (3) contemplative' (Betjeman, 1940: xiv). Whilst convenient, such a demarcation not only creates difficulties for the modern-day reader wishing to chart the evolution of the poet across time but also does not allow for the cross-over that can exist within individual poems. As a case in point, it fails to appreciate how many of Newbolt's more obviously patriotic poems were not simply bellicose jingoism but were simultaneously nostalgic seeking as they did to locate the origins of the best virtues of Englishness in forms of inherited tradition.

This new edition seeks then to rectify earlier misreadings by approaching Newbolt's work chronologically and drawing on material from all of his published volumes. In order of publication these were *Admirals All* (1897), *The Island Race* (1898), *The Sailing of the Long-Ships* (1902), *Songs of Memory and Hope* (1909), *St. George's Day* (1918) and the posthumously published *A Perpetual Memory* (1939). It also includes a selection of the poems added to *Poems New and Old* (effectively a Collected Works, which went through a number of editions) as well as a volume of children's verse published under the pseudonym of Henry Nemo entitled *Goodchild's Garland: Diversions and Perversions* (1909). This latter has been described as an 'enchanting little book of unexpected quirks and fancies, which includes a ballad about a parson and a badger, several re-told nursery rhymes, a humorous Christmas carol, and even a limerick' (Jackson, 1994: 133) and its inclusion here, in full, serves to show another side to the outwardly austere Newbolt. An appendix offers brief notes for many of the individual poems including details of provenance and explanations of historical allusions and references.

Early Life and Expressions of Patriotism

Newbolt's early life has already been much covered by biographers (see Chitty, 1997; Dickinson, 1981; Gervais, 2004; and Winterbottom, 1986), as well as in the first volume of his own autobiography (1932), thus it is not necessary to discuss it in any great detail here. Suffice to say that he was born in 1862 in Bilston, Staffordshire, of which his father, already on his second marriage – to Newbolt's mother – was vicar. (He was to die of cancer aged 42 in 1866.) Following a brief period of local education, Newbolt *fils* was sent away to a small school at Caistor on the Wolds in Lincolnshire that was run by the Reverend Anthony Bower, a Cambridge mathematician who had previously been a university tutor to Newbolt's father. Despite being hopeful of a scholarship to one of the more elite public schools (Eton or Winchester) Newbolt was forced instead to settle for Clifton College in Bristol and he and his mother moved to the city in 1876. Something of Newbolt's early schooling and character can be gleaned from a reading of his 1911 novel *The Twymans* in which the protagonist Percival Twyman is described as loving 'all games – cricket above the rest: but he had an equally strong taste for the reading of poetry, of which he assimilated enormous quantities, and the mysteries of heraldry, which expressed for him a whole rainbow of feelings and ideas' (Newbolt, 1911: 2). That young Twyman was a thinly veiled doppelgänger of his creator is obvious (the novel was subtitled, *A Novel of Youth*) and these interests, heraldry especially, were to remain dear to Newbolt throughout his life. In particular, the attributes developed through playing games (sportsmanship, respect for rules, physical courage), as well as the importance of lineage, ancestry, and tradition, were to become entwined together and combined into a world view which had what could crudely be called 'right conduct' at its heart.

Although Newbolt did not board at Clifton – his mother had taken a house opposite the Close – he nevertheless partook fully in the social life of the school. More importantly, it was also where his early interest in literature, and poetry especially, was fully awakened. Partly this was a result of the scholarship he had obtained; it was customary for such boys to study Latin and Greek whilst the school's extensive library meant young students had the opportunity, should they wish, to read the works of Keats and the still-living Tennyson. In addition, the Manx poet T.E. Brown was one of the school's masters, and it was through his encouragement that for the first time Newbolt began to write verse, some of which was published in the school magazine. Newbolt was to remember fondly the time spent with his former tutor: 'I was now and then a guest at his [Brown's] table, and admired the broad full-flowing stream of his conversation - it was even fuller than his letters. His bodily presence matched it - he rolled into the room, the Close or the School Chapel like a deep flood on an incoming tide' (Newbolt, 1932: 51–52).

Aside from his time at the school stimulating him creatively, it was at Clifton that Newbolt first encountered the public-school spirit which he was to so eloquently articulate and champion later in life. As David Turner tells us, such a spirit consisted of placing primacy on the building of good character and physique. These attributes were often developed through games playing which, in the manner of Plato's *Republic* and *Laws*, ensured that any 'display of physical activity would ... form[ed] one of the criteria for selection as members of the [Athenian] ruling class' (Turner, 2015: 100). At Clifton in particular these assumptions seem to have been especially prevalent: 'The School was ruled by a great Headmaster [John Percival] and served by teachers of distinction: it was vigorous, healthy, successful in academic work and games. Such a place was bound to make a deep impression upon those whose most formative years were spent there' (Winterbottom, 1986: 25). This claim is given support when one traces the future paths of Newbolt's contemporaries, who included Francis Younghusband, Douglas Haig, Arthur Quiller-Couch, and Roger Fry, all of whom in one way or another were to embody something of the Clifton ethos whether in exploration, the military, or the arts. Newbolt's affection for Clifton, though, seems to have run deepest of all. Even when, later in life, it seemed as if the world he knew was in danger of unravelling, his *alma mater* remained a point by which to anchor himself and he produced a number of poems in its honour as well as becoming President of the Old Cliftonian Society.

From Clifton, Newbolt won a Classical Scholarship to Corpus Christi College, Oxford, where he began to demonstrate both a deeper engagement with politics as well as his lifelong gift for attracting friends from across the intellectual spectrum. At Oxford these included the novelist Anthony Hope and the future Archbishop of Canterbury Cosmo Lang, as well as his tutor, the noted classical scholar Adam Sidgwick.

INTRODUCTION

Tellingly, Newbolt's autobiography is peppered with the names of the many eminent people he met, his dinner companions, and the country houses he visited; he was, throughout his life, always to be thought of as an excellent and welcome guest who relished hearty conversation. In other ways, though, his four undergraduate years were unremarkable. At that time Corpus was not one of Oxford's grander colleges and, despite his First in Honour Mods, he did not obtain a subsequent Fellowship, nor did he win any of the University prizes, and he appears to have made little mark at either the Union or within college sporting life. Of greatest significance perhaps was his continued production of poetry, although, as Patric Dickinson has noted, much of this early verse, which he had begun at school, was derivative, being 'Arthurian in matter and Tennysonian in manner' (Dickinson, 1981: 14). An example of this was the privately published *A Fair Death*, a medieval-inspired piece in forty rhyme royal stanzas. Whilst this and his first novel *Taken from the Enemy* (published four years later in 1892) are today barely remembered, they nevertheless marked the first showing of the themes of heroism, honour, and chivalry which were occupying an ever more central place in his way of thinking. Newbolt even went as far as to have his family coat of arms painted on a shield.

Leaving Oxford in 1885, Newbolt took up residency in London, where he started working in the law, first for his cousin's chambers, then afterwards at Lincoln's Inn, before qualifying fully as a barrister two years later. Such work suited the punctilious side to his character, especially given that 'Conveyancing rather than pleading … took up the greater part of his time' (Chitty, 1997: 73–74). Aside from the usual rounds of social engagements and theatre shows expected of a young and connected man about town, he also volunteered at a number of boys' clubs in the East End and then Notting Hill, in the process garnering a healthy respect for the independence of the working-class lads: 'they were intelligible, admirable and lovable human beings and I felt … that our life, on both sides, had become a different thing by the mere fact of our coming together. Certainly they enlarged my idea of patriotism, and when I had to leave them I found nothing to replace them' (Newbolt, 1932: 154). Although such statements could be read as paternalistic, Newbolt was undoubtedly sincere in the work he undertook and there is no doubting his horror and sadness at the squalid living conditions he observed. These experiences further convinced him of the rightness of the Liberal cause – part of which was in providing a legislative safety net for those who had fallen through society's cracks – and should in the process serve to disabuse us of the notion that Newbolt could never understand those 'ordinary' sailors and soldiers about whom he was to write.

The philanthropic work ceased however after his marriage in August 1889 to Margaret Duckworth, whom he had met whilst visiting Somerset. His autobiography recalls their initial meeting in which she appeared with 'a straw hat with a lilac satin ribbon, and with a basket full of grapes on her arm' (Newbolt, 1932: 164). Her family owned the large estate of Orchardleigh Park near Frome (which was to become a regular retreat for Newbolt later in life) and her mother was the daughter of John Campbell, 1st Baron Campbell, the former Lord Chancellor, a man best known for having been the principal sponsor of the 1857 Obscene Publications Act. Margaret, therefore, had a number of personal connections, two particularly important ones being her cousin Ella Coltman and her friend Mary Coleridge, the great-grandniece of Samuel Taylor. They had previously been part of a London literary group called the Grecians, learning Ancient Greek under William Johnson Cory (the unnamed dedicatee of 'Ionicus'), and this network provided an entrée for Newbolt to begin to properly advance his own burgeoning ambitions. Now calling themselves The Settee, the four of them all composed poems and stories which they read to each other on regular afternoons. They also attempted to collaborate on romantic novels, a chapter each. The dynamic was further strengthened – or perhaps complicated – by their entangled sexual relationships: Mary was a lesbian in love with Margaret, whilst Ella, having previously been involved with Margaret, begun her own (fully requited) relationship with Henry. For the rest of his life he was to effectively have two separate lovers and households.

Such extra-curricular activities did not however serve to diminish his productivity. Following another privately printed long verse-drama, *Mordred* – once again on an Arthurian theme although an improvement on *A Fair Death* – came the first recognizably Newboltian poem, 'Admirals All', which appeared anonymously in Andrew Lang's *Longman's Magazine* in 1895. Its opening stanza, evoking a panoply of naval heroes, set a suitably belligerent tone and marked the triumphal entry of a new voice into English poetry:

EFFINGHAM, Grenville, Raleigh, Drake,
   Here's to the bold and free!
Benbow, Collingwood, Byron, Blake,
   Hail to the Kings of the Sea!

INTRODUCTION

> Admirals all, for England's sake,
>   Honour be yours and fame!
> And honour, as long as waves shall break,
>   To Nelson's peerless name! ('Admirals All', lines 1–8)

Having now found his subject – 'San Stefano' about the sinking of a French brig moored off the Tuscan coast was next – Newbolt followed up with 'Drake's Drum', which was printed initially in *The St. James's Gazette* on 15 January 1896. The catalyst for this poem was the 'Kruger Telegram' incident in which nationalist sentiment had been stoked by an offer of support from the Germans to the troublesome Boers with whom Britain was soon again to be at war. Unquestionably amongst Newbolt's very best pieces, as well as being one of the most quoted in the entire canon, 'Drum's' particular strengths and allusions are so well known as to not need reiterating. Indeed, its familiarity is such that it is hard today to look at it anew and appreciate quite how arresting a poem it is. Whilst its sentiments may now be unfashionable, as a distillation of duty and courage it has few equals and, tellingly, all contemporary reviewers were to single it out for praise with some even then being convinced of its place in posterity. William Archer, for instance, was to call it 'one of the best sea songs in the language' (Archer, 1902: 292) whilst Robert Buchanan was to write that this 'magnificent song' will 'ensure him [Newbolt] a place in all future anthologies' (Buchanan, 1899: 266). The Devonian dialect sounds are convincing especially when read aloud, the use of assonance adds the necessary propulsion, and Vanessa Jackson's accurate assessment that these features 'give the poem its very compact and contained structural feeling, but also its pace and energy' (Jackson, 1994: 74) are testament to the meticulous nature of Newbolt the poetic craftsman.

Another to be impressed with 'Drake's Drum' was fellow poet Robert Bridges who, upon first reading it in manuscript, was said to have remarked to its author, '"You'll not write anything better than that – it isn't given to man to write anything better than that. I wish I had ever written anything half so good"' (Bridges quoted in Newbolt, 1932: 187). Apocryphal or not, Bridges soon passed the word to Laurence Binyon who was in the process of editing a series of pamphlets called *Elkin Matthews' Shilling Garland*, which were intended to showcase the work of emerging authors. Suitably impressed himself with this new find, Binyon set about gathering together all of Newbolt's extant poems with the little book that he fittingly entitled *Admirals All* being first published on 21 October 1897, a date which coincided with the anniversary of the Battle of Trafalgar. Newbolt's was the eighth in the *Shilling Garland* series to appear, following others by Bridges, Richard Watson Dixon, Margaret Woods, and Stephen Phillips and he later declared that he had been 'wearied daily with answering congratulations [and] replying to questions' (Newbolt, 1932: 197). The connection to Trafalgar, whilst unintended, was, however, especially apt as half of the pamphlet's dozen poems were concerned with naval life and its heroes, most notably Sir Francis Drake (as we have seen) but also Lord Hawke and the Fighting Temeraire ship, which had previously been rendered memorably in paint by Turner.

Despite its humble beginnings and slender size, and notwithstanding the comparative obscurity of its author, within two weeks *Admirals* had gone through four editions. In the next year this was to increase to over twenty editions, some with further poems added, which led to sales in excess of 20,000 copies. Such extraordinary numbers were matched only by the tone of the reviews, nearly all of which were commensurately positive; one for example was moved to comment that the book had 'a certain freshness, a simple emphasis, an oratorical ability, which are decidedly agreeable qualities' (*The Athenaeum*, 22 January 1898: 111), whilst another was to acknowledge a 'proud and spirited and inspiring little book' (*The Speaker*, 11 December 1897: 668). Furthermore, its author was regarded as one who had 'spirit and force, and who employs them in proclaiming the very sound doctrine that the safety of England depends upon a strong Navy' (*The Times*, 5 November 1897: 13).

This critical success was repeated a year later with *The Island Race* (1898) which not only included the poems from *Admirals All* but also added 28 new ones. As with its predecessor some of the best were on naval themes ('Admiral Death', 'Messmates', 'The Death of Admiral Blake' stand out), but to these were now added a fresh strand of poems addressing school and school life ('Clifton Chapel', 'The Echo'). That there were few surprises in its subject matter, and with Newbolt on the type of terrain he had previously mastered, explains why *Island Race* too received good notice. It is, however, telling that some reviewers were by now beginning to hint at the problems which would dog Newbolt in the future: 'The imperialist fervour is always there, but it is not always sublimated into poetic inspiration … he really must learn to distinguish what is poetry from what is merely politics' (*The Academy*, 3 December 1898: 371). Nevertheless, Newbolt was now one of the most well-known poets in the land and his success meant that he could leave the Bar and devote himself full-time to writing. Indeed, it would not be stretching a point to say that these two books, published (and mostly written) in the space of a year, made their author famous almost overnight and, on sheer sales alone, must rank as amongst the most significant volumes of the period.

To what, however, can such startling popularity be attributed? That there was clearly a ready-made market for the type of poetry Newbolt could produce is undeniable; this is made apparent when we remember that many of the poems in *Admirals All* had been previously published in widely read and respected journals in Britain and America. As has been noted, the title poem first appeared in *Longman's Magazine* three years earlier, with other poems being printed in subsequent months across a range of periodicals. More broadly, such receptivity was, as Julia Stapleton has acutely observed, a result of the emergence of a '"nationalization" of culture and patriotism, rooted in the enhanced self-consciousness of the English people, that gathered pace after 1870' (Stapleton, 1998: 243). As one contemporary was to put it, 'He [Newbolt] brings to his task a fine enthusiasm for heroism … and the true *English point of view*' (*The Academy*, 30 October 1897: 371, italics added). This point has also been reiterated by Stefan Collini (1991), who alluded to the growth amongst public intellectuals – Collini pays particular attention to James Fitzjames Stephen and Henry Fawcett, but we might also here include Newbolt – of a more masculine conception of liberty. Such a view meant not merely triumphing over adversity but, where necessary, stoically accepting defeat and setback. Playing the game, indeed.

Within this milieu could also be placed (and in the process, demonstrating the point made above) such other examples as Kipling, W.E. Henley, and even Alfred Austin. In the latter's case, continued production of execrable xenophobic doggerel was no barrier to gaining the Laureateship, whilst even Henley, a Victorian literary titan and revolutionary in many other respects, could get so carried away as to use a sharpened sword as a metaphorical instrument of ferocious pseudo-Darwinian intent, designed for 'Sifting the nations,/ The slag from the metal,/ The waste and the weak/ From the fit and the strong' ('The Song of the Sword', lines 127–130, in Henley, 1892). Lines like this do Henley's reputation a disservice (although he had a well-cultivated nasty streak) and few other writers would have dared be so forthright in using such explicit language, which appeared to suggest in no uncertain terms that there was a hierarchy of nations with Britain at the apex. That being said, this did not preclude there being a wider sense that she still had a governing role to play in world affairs, one driven by a divinely-inspired sense of mission. No one invoked this more boldly than Kipling in his infamous entreaty of the 'White Man's Burden' in which those 'enlightened' nations were implored to 'Send forth the best ye breed' to 'Fill full the mouth of Famine/ And bid the sickness cease' ('The White Man's Burden', lines 19–20, in Kipling, 1903). Likewise, William Watson (another forgotten figure despite being briefly Kipling's equal in popularity) hinted at the *Christian* element to this 'civilizing' process in his sonnet sequence *The Purple East* (1896), which attacked Britain's abandonment of the Armenian Christians at the hands of the neighbouring Ottoman Empire. Although more historically rooted and drawing less obviously on contemporary political events, Newbolt too was to capture this mood. In his poem 'The Vigil', for instance, he invoked England as a place where 'the sacred flame/ Burns before the inmost shrine,/ Where the lips that love thy name/ Consecrate their hopes and thine' ('The Vigil', lines 1–4), whilst the poem's refrain of 'Pray that God defend the Right' struck the right notes of manifest national destiny. Long after its publication, these lines continued to embody something of a wider national feeling and this is reinforced by a note from its author in which he claimed that the poem was 'being quoted, sung, recited and reprinted from one end of the country to the other, and I have letters of thanks by every post' (Newbolt, note to self, 8 August 1914, quoted in Margaret Newbolt, 1942: 190).

As emboldened as these and other such verses may have been, it nevertheless behoves us to remember that, at the time, a complex system of foreign alliances and entanglements had led to a state of precariousness in political and diplomatic affairs. The best known of these centred upon the scramble for imperial territory in Africa. Given the obvious potential this created for conflict and skirmish, a feeling of latent unease had grown in Britain, one that would have been felt most keenly amongst the readers of Newbolt's poetry, who were, in the main, increasingly politically aware, a happy consequence of the improvements to state education and greater accessibility of the popular press. Assuaging these anxieties, therefore, became an important aspect to Newbolt's poetry: 'It seems likely, too, that one of the reasons for the success of *Admirals All* was that its content spoke to the need of many of its readers for certainty and faith in an age of increasing doubt and questioning' (Jackson, 1994: 77). The Boer War was a case in point; necessary it may have been, yet the protracted and draining nature of the conflict, including the famous sieges of Ladysmith and

INTRODUCTION

Mafeking, resulted in an overwhelming majority for the Conservatives and their Liberal Unionist allies in the 1900 'Khaki' election. As Paul Readman has shown, not only was there a large element of jingoist rhetoric surrounding the election campaigning, but also 'significant numbers of the *ordinary people* of Britain were interested in imperial and patriotic issues bearing little relation to the humdrum realities of their daily lives' (Readman, 2001: 136, italics added). Although, as we shall later see, Newbolt's response to these events was to betray his own feelings of ambiguity, there would nevertheless have been something continually reassuring about those earlier poems which connected their readership back to a more glorious age in which 'they left us a kingdom none can take—/ The realm of the circling sea,/ To be ruled by the rightful sons of Blake,/ And the Rodneys yet to be' ('Admirals All', lines 49–52). In a similar vein, a poem such as 'The Volunteer' seemed designed, in its dozen short lines, to allay any concerns that courage – and instinctive courage, at that – was a feature lacking amongst the defenders of empire:

> "HE leapt to arms unbidden,
>   Unneeded, over-bold;
> His face by earth is hidden,
>   His heart in earth is cold.
>
> "Curse on the reckless daring
>   That could not wait the call,
> The proud fantastic bearing
>   That would be first to fall!"
>
> O tears of human passion,
>   Blur not the image true;
> This was not folly's fashion,
>   This was the man we knew.   ('The Volunteer', lines 1–12)

Clearly then, the sentiments found within Newbolt's early poems chimed with various populist moods and there was a sense of deliberate orchestration by the press who carefully printed and reprinted them in their newspapers as such wider anxieties waxed and waned. Nevertheless, far from such verses being regressive and atavistic, a more careful reading of the literary landscape surrounding these early volumes should serve to position them as a counterweight – maybe even a *counter-reaction* – to other contemporary literary trends and fashions. In referring to those wider coteries, which usually aspired to be more obviously highbrow,

Vanessa Jackson once again rightly tells us that 'there was a surfeit of escapist romance and drooping lilies and roses being published in books, pamphlets, periodicals, and newspapers at that time ... Poetic language in the hands of a host of Pre-Raphaelite camp followers and would-be-aesthetes had tended to become cloying, precious, and overly ornate, while the subject matter was often viewed as sentimental and trivial' (Jackson, 1994: 68). Indeed, it is worth remembering that other volumes published in the same year as *Admirals All* included Arthur Symons' *Amoris Victima*, John Davidson's *New Ballads* and Francis Thompson's *New Poems*. Oscar Wilde too might well have had Newbolt's verses in his thoughts when dismissing patriotism as 'the virtue of the vicious' and as 'only the virtue of small minds' (Wilde quoted in Cooper-Prichard, 1931: 20 and 99). Although we should be wary of inferring too much from reported throwaway aphorisms, it nevertheless speaks to the emergence of a poetical divide between, on the one hand, those foppish and flowery forms of aesthetic writing which encompassed Symbolism and Decadence and, on the other, a more obviously masculine form of versifying which had public and political concerns at its heart. This was not always a neat divide; the pugnacious W.E. Henley, for instance, was very modern in much of his writing (especially his *In Hospital* sequence) whilst, by contrast, the arch-aesthete Swinburne's controversial poem 'Transvaal' spewed forth rabid anti-Boer feeling ('scourge these dogs agape with jaws afoam,/ Down out of life. Strike, England, and strike home'). Nevertheless, for all of the difficulties of demarcation, what can be said with certainty was that there was a clear place for the sort of 'salt and racy' (Sampson in *The Bookman*, November 1914: 36) poetry that characterized the early work of Newbolt and which was, through its wide circulation, gradually beginning to gain the ascendency.

To view Newbolt's popularity simply as a consequence of a prevailing mood of bellicosity and attendant populist feeling is, however, to pay insufficient regard to both the skill and depth of his highly original talent as well as his instinctive sense of the sound and rhythm of a poem. Nor does it recognize how his verses, in tandem with his other literary works, formed part of a deeply-held philosophy of action which centred upon notions of heroism and tradition. In that respect, it would be wrong to suggest that Newbolt's use of historical figures – Nelson, Hawke, Blake, and the rest – was arbitrary or designed for easy popular appeal so as to provide an echo chamber for his readership. Rather, these men very deliberately 'represented active patriots in the Elizabethan tradition' (Jackson, 1994: 39), that is to say, those such as Drake who

INTRODUCTION

were ready at a moment's notice to serve the needs of their country: 'I'll quit the port o' Heaven,/ An' drum them up the Channel as we drummed them long ago' ('Drake's Drum', lines 15–16). Obeying such a call when it came was one of the key virtues that Newbolt believed was central to living a worthwhile and principled life. For him, these virtues had their origins in the medieval past and were best exemplified by the valour and courage of ancient knights who had been bound together by bonds of honour and fraternal association. Public schools and, in particular, their games playing provided the modern-day equivalent: 'The public school ... has derived the housemaster from the knight to whose castle boys were sent as pages ... prefects, from the senior squires or "masters of the henchman" ... and the love of games, the "sporting" or "amateur" view of them, from tournaments and the chivalric rules of war' (Newbolt, 1917: vii). Today, with the nature of what it means to be patriotic having changed, such a view may strike us as somewhat elitist, yet, as Mark Girouard tells us, 'in the sense that Victorians selected the qualities which they most admired in chivalry and remodelled games in the light of them, he [Newbolt] was saying no more than the truth' (Girouard, 1981: 235). Much of this remodelling was undertaken through fiction; in the case of Newbolt, his retelling of Froissart's chronicles as well as the novels *The Old Country* (1906) and *Aladore* (1914) were set in medieval times and deliberately intended as vehicles by which to impute the modern temperament into the past. So explicit was this intent that one reviewer was moved to comment that 'Mr. Newbolt desired to demonstrate that our ancestors of the Middle Ages were very much like ourselves' (*The Athenaeum*, 8 December 1906: 730).

Of course, Newbolt was hardly the first to do this. Ironically, given their place as forerunners of Symbolism – an artistic movement which provided inspiration for the sort of effete verse which sat at the opposite end of the spectrum to Newbolt – it was previous generations of Pre-Raphaelite artists from Dante Gabriel Rossetti to Edward Burne-Jones who had initially sounded this note through their illustrations of Arthurian stories and the inspiration they drew from such texts as Thomas Malory's *Le Morte d'Arthur*. Tennyson's poems too were part of their collective canon and, in 'The Lady of Shallot', 'Sir Galahad', and, most important of all, the *Idylls of the King* sequence, Arthur and his court were held to be archetypes of male-bonded Christian nobility who served as embodiments of the highest forms of integrity and, therefore, as models for contemporary Victorian society. Arthur in particular was to be equated with such latter-day heroes as Prince Albert and the Duke of Wellington. However, for all of Tennyson's sparkling surface, there was much that was sentimental about his associations, a point made in Newbolt's *Mordred* (1895) which, despite being largely unread today, did nevertheless seek to correct what were seen as some of the earlier errors of the Laureate. In this instance, 'Arthur was not a "blameless king" but an incestuous adulterer' (Chitty, 1997: 99).

There was, therefore, a harder and less flowery edge to Newbolt's thinking around chivalry and heroism and he took umbrage at earlier bowdlerizations. Evidently, he was aware of the flaws of his heroes – Nelson too was an adulterer whilst Drake had flirted with piracy – and this awareness served to make them and their deeds more human and relatable. Such earthy appreciation also necessitated repudiating the views of intellectuals like Thomas Carlyle who envisioned the hero/Great Man as one armed with 'divine insight into the inner reality of existence' (Jackson, 1994: 39). By contrast, those whom Newbolt saw as worthy of admiration were less of the mind and more of the body; in other words, men 'primarily of action, whose selfless and courageous deeds ... provided an inspirational model to emulate' (Ibid., 40). Emulation here is an important term as Newbolt perceived heroism and the heroic character as one part of a broader national inheritance, beginning with medieval knights and descending down to Nelson via Drake, Blake, and Hawke and, finally, epitomized in contemporaries such as Jackie Fisher and Douglas Haig. All such men (and it was usually men) were driven by a sense of honour, fair play, and patriotic duty, which were ideals to be universally aspired to. In light of that, it was no coincidence that one of Newbolt's very best poems 'Minora Sidera' was dedicated to Leslie Stephen, the first editor of the *Dictionary of National Biography*. This in itself was an exhaustive project which sought to collate and record the achievements of those who, often without clamour, had made a meaningful contribution to their country through aspiring to the high ideals Newbolt so revered:

> Whether their fame centuries long should ring
>   They cared not over-much,
>   But cared greatly to serve God and the king,
>   And keep the Nelson touch;
>
> And fought to build Britain above the tide
>   Of wars and windy fate;
>   And passed content, leaving to us the pride
>   Of lives obscurely great.   ('Minora Sidera', lines 17–24)

INTRODUCTION

Understanding this precept and its centrality to Newbolt's thinking can thus not only help in informing our reading of some of those early lyrics which had heroism at their core but also, in the process, move us away from those interpretations which have continued to see such poems as little more than exuberant displays of xenophobia. The three best examples, all from his first two collections, which embrace most obviously these ideas of chivalry, good conduct, and national tradition are 'He Fell Among Thieves', 'Clifton Chapel', and, most (in)famously of all, 'Vitaï Lampada'. Such is their importance in understanding the core of Newbolt's thinking, Susan Chitty has seen fit to label them as three of Newbolt's 'Big Four' (Chitty, 1997: 110) (the other of the quartet being 'Drake's Drum').

Any attempt to counter the derisory claims made about Newbolt, needs, however, initially to recognize that the imperial landscape of which his poetry was a part was far from homogeneous. Indeed, casually lumping together all writers who fall into this bracket has been the primary cause of much misunderstanding. Such a point is suggested by Malvern Van Wyck Smith, who, in citing poetic responses to the Boer War as a case in point, distinguished between 'those imbued with the activist fervours of the "Henley School"; those suffused with the exalted public school verities found in Sir Henry Newbolt's verse; and those declaiming a crusading, vitalist doctrine of war' (Van Wyck Smith, 1978: 42). Under this categorization, therefore, Newbolt's patriotic verses were never simplistic jingoism. That being said, they have served to cast a long shadow with 'Vitaï Lampada' in particular being the critics' weapon of choice by which to beat him whenever his name is mentioned. Partly, this was down to its popularity and, in that respect, it clearly rivalled 'Drake's Drum' as a poem known by those who may otherwise have never read any other poetry. As late as 1923, and in the midst of a lecture tour in Canada, Newbolt was to write in exasperation: 'As for Play up and play the Game - it's a kind of Frankenstein's Monster that I created thirty years ago and now I find it falling on my neck at every street corner! In vain do I explain what is poetry: they roar for "Play up"' (Newbolt, letter to Ella Coltman, 1 March 1923, quoted in Margaret Newbolt, 1942: 300). More seriously, the unease with which it has sat amongst subsequent generations readers lies in the way in which the first and the second stanzas so easily transition from the image of the cricket ground to that of a battlefield (and then back again) with the underlying assumption that both sport and warfare were impelled by the same hearty forces of public-school spirit and *esprit de corps*. Theatres of conflict were therefore reduced to nothing more than a grown-up version of the games field. That Newbolt chose to invoke them in the form of a rollicking ballad could hardly have helped. Little better, perhaps, was 'He Fell Among Thieves' which, according to Peter Hopkirk (1990), was inspired by the story of the adventurer and explorer George W. Hayward, who was captured and executed in modern-day Pakistan, then still part of India and one of the furthest flung parts of the British Empire. In Newbolt's tale the captured man is granted a reprieve of one night in which, during his broken sleep, he envisions the things dearest to him, including his old school, his Oxford College, and his local church, along with a memory of his father. Despite clearly being drawn from Newbolt's own life – the 'gray little church across the park,/ The mounds that hide the loved and honoured dead' ('He Fell Among Thieves', lines 21–22) describes Orchardleigh – once again it is possible to argue that the serious business of war and death has become trivialized. Is it little more than wishful thinking that a man facing imminent execution would find solace in such nostalgic flights of fancy?

However, as well as recognizing that these poems are, as has already been intimated, far removed from the more obviously chauvinistic and occasionally spiteful pieces of the period, three additional points of mitigation must be borne in mind. First, we must acknowledge the skill by which these and other poems were constructed. As a case in point, 'He Fell Among Thieves' is notable for employing a stanza structure which juxtaposes three long and reflective lines with a shorter final fourth line, which has the effect when read aloud of reinforcing the peril of the situation and the inevitability of the death to come. The peculiar placing of 'A sword swept' ('He Fell Among Thieves', line 47) creates a particularly effective diminuendo. Second, it further behoves us to remember that the views being put forward by Newbolt were far from uncommon at the time and, as such, his poems should be understood as a means by which he was able to channel a wider social *zeitgeist*. Lawrence James, for one, has rightly written that 'by making the battlefield the complement of the cricket pitch, Newbolt gave permanence to some of the deepest sentiments cherished by late-Victorian and Edwardian officers' (James, 1985: 159). After all, many of the officers defending the 'square that broke' ('Vitaï Lampada', line 10) had, like Newbolt, been through the public-school system and it was in their hallowed and ancient grounds and quads where such ideas of bravery and duty had been imprinted. One of the architects of this system of thought had been the Headmaster of Rugby, Thomas Arnold, and his first biographer recalls him telling the school's oldest boys that 'they should feel like officers in the army or navy, whose want of moral courage would indeed be thought cowardice' (Arnold quoted in Worboise, 1859: 62). Nor were such admonitions without good cause; as Newbolt revealed, 'I spent most of the years of my life under the certainty of war, the conviction that my country must pass through the trial of a great war; the necessary efforts of training for it the force and the thoughts of character' (Margaret Newbolt, 1942: 187).

Finally, and most importantly, these poems need to be read not as longings for colonial control or the maintenance of a strictly hierarchical or racially-oriented society but as comments on the historical heritability of virtues and behaviours. 'Vitaï Lampada', we should remember, translates as 'torch of life' and comes from Lucretius's *De Rerum Natura*, in which a torch was passed from one runner to the next. In so titling the poem, Newbolt was therefore envisioning it quite deliberately as a way by which he too could hand on to his readership the virtues he saw as important, ones which he had previously acquired at Clifton and which were central to living a good life. 'He Fell Among Thieves' mines a similar seam in that it lays down a blueprint for heroism; the protagonist is no coward and he faces death with a poise and equanimity which suggests not only his unflappable courage but also an unshakeable faith in God. That these values were here formed and forged in the relatively closed world of the public schools and so not accessible to a wider audience is, once more, to miss the point: 'Newbolt was using words and symbols that would already be familiar and accessible to a broad readership, for sporting expressions and images were in common use during the late-nineteenth and early twentieth centuries, occurring in parliamentary speeches, in newspaper articles, in periodical literature, in popular novels and poetry, and elsewhere' (Jackson, 1994: 84). These were then poems which held universal appeal and spoke to a longer historical tradition encompassing all men. As a case in point, a letter by H.J. Rose, an army chaplain, later published in *The Spectator*, talked of the inspiring effect that Newbolt's lines had on the common soldier: 'Over and over again, the sick man wasted by wounds and disease; the strong man, doomed to inaction on the lines of communication; the man at the very front, almost within range of the enemy's fire-has been nerved and cheered "to play the game", against all odds' (Rose quoted in *The Spectator*, 18 October 1902: 566).

That these poems as well as others within Newbolt's first two seminal volumes retained their popularity into the succeeding century is understandable; a reputation so rightly and rapidly gained would take a generation at least to be lost. They were, of course, very much of their time – that is, of the Victorian era – and they therefore gave loud voice to the many expectations and certainties which defined that period. In his way, 'Newbolt was merely being the practical patriot, seeking those words which … might help rather than harm action' (Grainger, 1986: 74). As the old century came to its end, however, so did that Victorian era give way to the Edwardian, a transition almost perfectly delineated by the commencement of the Second Anglo-Boer War (1899–1902), also known as the Boer War, itself a precursor to the total forms of warfare which were only a little over a decade away. Although these demarcations would not have been felt at the time, in retrospect it is possible to see how they marked a comparable shift in sentiment, one that would define the new reign. That shift was, once again, to both affect and be encapsulated by Newbolt, in the process broadening and enhancing him as a poet and a thinker. It is, therefore, to that transformation that the discussion now turns.

Changing Forms of Commemoration

The first major development in Newbolt's poetry came in his third book, *The Sailing of the Long-Ships* (1902). Of its 30 or so poems about half were concerned with war and its attendant sacrifices, with its moods and subject matter also spilling over into the volume which succeeded it – *Songs of Memory and Hope* (1909). The catalyst for this change in emphasis was, as we have mentioned, the Boer War (1899–1902), which was a subject impossible for Newbolt, by now the unofficial laureate of patriotism and whose books were outselling all of his rivals', to ignore. Given that this was his first event of any significance there was an expectation amongst the reading public that he would rise to the occasion, a point suggested by an immediate doubling of his book sales during this period as he strove to capture the wider sentiment. Initially, at least, he did not disappoint; November 1899 saw the first publication, this time in *The Spectator*, of the six stanzas comprising 'The Sailing of the Long-Ships', a poem which celebrated the embarkation of 50,000 troops to South Africa:

> THEY saw the cables loosened, they saw the gangways cleared,
> They heard the women weeping, they heard the men that cheered;
> Far off, far off, the tumult faded and died away,
> And all alone the sea-wind came singing up the Bay.
> ('The Sailing of the Long-Ships', lines 1–4)

INTRODUCTION

Drawing comparisons with Nelsonian times – Trafalgar and Cape St. Vincent are mentioned in later stanzas – the poem ends with the by now inevitable invocation of national tradition and the passing on of virtue: 'Mark as ye go the beacons that woke the world with light/ When down their ancient highway your fathers passed to fight' (Ibid., lines 23–24). However, whilst such sentiments traversed familiar Newbolt terrain, and are as well articulated here as ever, they were not to define the rest of his poetry during these years, with the turn of contemporary events dictating a shifting in his emphasis. This change was subtle yet can be seen in the brief, uncollected, and easily missed epigraph that preceded the main body of poems:

> I that twined a wreath for olden splendour -
>   Drake and Blake and Nelson's mighty name -
> Come again to deck with flowers more tender
>   New-made graves of unaccomplished fame.

As Michael Bright has pointed out, 'Commemoration of heroic sacrifice is still Newbolt's main purpose, but these poetic wreaths bedeck the "new-made graves" of the Boer War rather than pay tribute to "olden splendour"' (Bright, 1990: 157). In other words, although Newbolt's poetry was still concerned with annunciating the themes of courage, heroism, and sacrifice, the dominant mood was now to be one of elegy rather than of celebration; Victorian pomp giving way to Edwardian reflection. Whilst the continuing war may have provided the immediate context, we can also identify a number of wider aspects which served to nudge him in this direction. First, Newbolt's entrenchment within Liberal Party politics – he was by this point editor of *The Monthly Review* – meant that he was obligated to make public comment on wider events and, with some reservations, he was therefore bound to go along with party leader Henry Campbell-Bannerman's criticism of the prosecution of the conflict. Generals, such as the widely castigated Redvers Buller, were not perhaps to blame personally for the incompetent handling of the fighting, but they were nonetheless ripe to be held up as products of a rotten civilization that had served to erode those attributes Newbolt so cherished: 'The admiration of wealth, however acquired, and of rank, however gained or inherited; the fatty degeneration caused by indolence and self-indulgence – these are the diseases which threaten the Empire, whether in war or in peace' (Newbolt, 1902a: 7). Such sentiments pepper Newbolt's writing at this time, particularly his regular *Review* editorials, and his critique of the war tied to a broader appreciation of the changing shape of the empire. Whilst supportive of the imperial principle his caveat was that it should 'be built up peacefully and without sacrificing small nationalities, and provided the civilised parts of it are given local self-government' (Newbolt, 1900: 5). Any poetic shifts were thus reciprocated and mirrored in broader, exigent political thinking.

The second aspect to impact Newbolt, and one of perhaps still greater importance, was the effects of the war on the alumni of Clifton College with whom he was, as ever, closely associated. A glance through the archives of *The Old Cliftonian* magazine indicates the extent to which the school had become involved with the October 1899 edition mentioning the names of 85 young men who had recently set out for South Africa. Five months later this figure had risen to over 200. In all, Derek Winterbottom has calculated that 'the total number was to be 347, almost all officers' (Winterbottom, 1986: 53), with many ultimately losing their lives. Stung into action, Newbolt's response was a quartet of school-centred poems including, from 1899, 'The School Fellow' and 'The Best School of All' and, from May 1901, 'The School at War', in which, in a manner comparable to the prisoner in 'He Fell Among Thieves', an army asleep before battle dreams of more carefree times: 'We played again the immortal games,/ And grappled with the fierce old friends,/ And cheered the dead undying names,/ And sang the song that never ends' ('The School at War', lines 13–16). These were followed by 'Commemoration' in July of the same year.

In seeking to understand Newbolt's thinking at this time, further consideration really needs to be given to this small group of school verses as no better barometer exists for determining his shifting sensibilities. Whilst we cannot doubt the workmanship or the genuineness of feeling which lay behind the works, the first three of the poems mentioned above nevertheless served to reinforce the received impression of Newbolt as one who not only glorified sacrifice but also ran the risk of cheapening such loss of life by filtering it through the lens of a formal public-school code of honour and fair play. As Cecil Eby puts it, the boys in poems such as these were being elevated to the status of 'a sort of Nietzschean *Übermensch* wielding a cricket bat instead of a club' (Eby, 1987: 99). And was it not verging on parody to suggest that the young combatants were 'weary and cheery' ('The School Fellow', line 8) driven as they were by the ethic of '"As fair a fight, as clear as sun"' (Ibid., line 10)? Furthermore, from a stylistic perspective, although these poems clearly echo some of the more patently patriotic verses of his previous books which have already been discussed, their narrow focus precludes them from standing amongst Newbolt's best pieces. Unlike 'He Fell Among Thieves' and 'Vitaï Lampada' the sense here is that they are too obviously 'public school poems' and also too closely attenuated to the context of Clifton to carry the necessary message of universality.

Such an assessment cannot however be applied to the seminal 'Commemoration', the last of this little group to be written, and a poem conceived as a direct response to the muted end-of-term school celebrations at which the list of casualties had been too long to read out. Here, then, was the tipping point. Gone fully now was the previous bombast and cheerful sacrifice in the name of school, monarch, and country; instead, the opening lines invoke, to these eyes at least, the quiet Classical contemplation of Gray's famous 'Elegy' (the 'granite pillar' suggests too a portrait by Romney or Reynolds) and there is something approaching that heightened sense of rumination and stasis as the poem moves its way solemnly yet inexorably forward. Paul Webb has sympathetically written of Newbolt's Christianity that it was 'of the muscular variety – though he was both more thoughtful and more intelligent than this may imply' (Webb, 1987: 55) and such a claim seems especially apt in this context as the sense of loss is not only here dealt with in a more direct way than before but also betrays a sensitivity and intensity with which Newbolt is rarely credited. The young men being addressed are no longer simple, archetypal, anonymous embodiments of chivalry but living potentials of flesh and blood whose lives have been brutally cut short; war is no longer an abstract concept, far from land and mind, but a brutalizing and difficult force with human implications.

Adding to this, as Kenneth Millard points out: '["Commemoration"] is excellently restrained, it avoids explicit statement and succeeds by indirection, transfiguring its meaning into the final image "as drifted leaves on an endless plain"' (Millard, 1991: 34). This is indeed a fine image that suggests the transience of youth as the boys pass out from the school having heard perhaps their final sermon, one which is given added poignancy when noting the context in which it was written. Such a mood is further suggested in lines 5 and 6 where not only is the theme of loss further reinforced ('when the place was still unhaunted') but so is the uncertainty of the transition into adulthood ('the strangest tale in the world was still untold'). The poem's particular strength resides, therefore, both in its accurate capture of the public-school landscape through allusions to architecture, chapels, and sermons for those on the cusp of becoming men but also in the ambiguity which surrounds the middle lines of the final stanza – 'And I longed to hear them speak of the word that was said,/ But I knew that I longed in vain' ('Commemoration', lines 33–34). Superficially this could be read as the poet's/Newbolt's sadness and sense of loss over the fact that he recognizes all that remains to him of the boys is a transient memory and that their death is an imminent possibility. If, however, we place an emphasis upon the first of the two lines we encounter a more profound reading and one which thereby elevates the poem above its companions. We now understand this as a shift away from the poet to the boys as we are asked to consider what they themselves would make or would have made of the 'word that was said' (Ibid., line 33); in other words, asking their thoughts on the sermon which has just been delivered. Are these their thoughts on the obligations of duty as pointed out within the fourth stanza, or is Newbolt here referring to the following stanza, which suggests a guiding of the soul after death? If the former, could this be construed as Newbolt offering a criticism of the assumption that public-school boys were expected unthinkingly to prove themselves through heroism and chivalry? Or is he instead calling into question his own faith, which to that point had been that of a regular Church of England man with a belief in the afterlife accepted equally unquestioningly? These questions are not made explicit – and we cannot easily decode Newbolt's intentions – however they can be read into the work and their presence says something about the agnostic and epochal quality of the poem, one which ranks amongst his finest and which best embodies the shift in emphasis referred to above.

For all of its ambiguity, however, we should not see this as an anti-war poem nor was Newbolt ever to be an anti-war poet. Nevertheless, caveats aside, it does hint, as we shall see, at some of the questions which were to bedevil him over a decade later during the First World War, especially the extent to which fighting, even that in support of a just cause, could and should ever be glorified in verse. The difference between Newbolt's earlier role as a purveyor of glory and the realities of what such glory involved thus represented a newly found tension in his work, one which came to be increasingly important from this point on. Some of his own reservations may have been driven by a wider social awareness, with the events of the Boer War having placed into stark relief the poor health of much of the population – those about and for whom he wrote. In particular, the 1904 Committee on Physical Deterioration, reporting after the resolution to the conflict, found that four out of ten men who had signed up to fight had been turned away, a consequence of a range of physical ailments including malnutrition, stunted growth, and rickets. As Bernard Semmel (1960) and others since have speculated, governmental findings of this kind led to wide-ranging questions being asked as to how it would be possible in the future to sustain and preserve an empire given this prevalence of general ill-health. Such concerns would surely have alarmed Newbolt and they were to act as a catalyst for many of his beloved Liberal Party's social reforms in the following years, including the introduction of national insurance, old-age pensions, school medical checks, and the 'Children's Charter'.

Of course, having sympathy with the plight of the working man was nothing new; Kipling's fictional Tommy Atkins from his best-selling *Barrack-Room Ballads* (1892), for instance, had served as a cipher for his genuine concern with the fate of the soon-to-be-demobbed working-class soldier, a connection that may well have been in David Daiches' mind when referring to Newbolt as Kipling's 'well-dressed shadow' (Daiches, 1940, 22). However, whilst Newbolt and Kipling shared similarities during the 1890s, by the time of the Boer War in late 1899 their forms of patriotism were beginning to diverge. J.H. Grainger for one has made clear that 'Newbolt's almost sacramental English patriotism, lofty, deliberate, enlightened, was quite distinct from that of Kipling' (Grainger, 1986: 76) and he further points to the Boer War as a time when 'he [Newbolt] began to have doubts about England as the nursery of those virtues which the Empire and the world needed' (Ibid., 77). As Kipling's patriotism was therefore sustained by looking for the enemies within – usually those of a liberal/Liberal persuasion – Newbolt began to turn away from the trope of heroism to become more reflective and inward-looking. This new feeling was captured in 'April on Waggon Hill', written in 1900 (although for some reason not collected in book form until 1910), which was an elegiac poem addressing a Devon soldier killed in battle:

> LAD, and can you rest now,
>   There beneath your hill?
> Your hands are on your breast now,
>   But is your heart so still?
> 'Twas the right death to die, lad,
>   A gift without regret,
> But unless truth's a lie, lad,
>   You dream of Devon yet.   ('April on Waggon Hill', lines 1–8)

With its distinctive rhythm and reference to the 'lad' there are obvious echoes here of A.E. Housman, a connection that is further reflected in the spare and quiet simplicity of 'A Sower' in which 'the dumb fields/ Desire his tread,/ And no earth yields/ A wheat more red' ('A Sower', lines 13–16). Newbolt, one feels, could not have failed to notice the popularity of *A Shropshire Lad,* whose pleasing combination of nostalgia and pastoralism accounted for its recent boost in sales. Key to both of these poems, however, as well as in the previously discussed 'Commemoration', were the dominant moods of loss and departure and in 'The Only Son' the theme is extended with the perfectly pitched last two lines signifying deep maternal loss, an aspect unusual in Newbolt: '"*Within her heart she rocks a dead child, crying/ 'My son, my little son'*"' ('The Only Son', lines 15–16, italics in original). Brooks and Faulkner are, in light of that, astute in observing that such poems 'try ... to grapple with the personal costs of dying for the Empire, costs that are registered far less abstractly in any of his pre-war poems' (Brooks and Faulkner, 1996: 44).

That Newbolt could so competently assimilate the style of Housman – and also Hardy, whose own war poetry often focused on those left behind and their sense of alienation – is itself suggestive of the greater range of forms and subject matter which he now sought to cultivate. Another example of this is in the short 'The Viking's Song':

> WHEN I thy lover first
>   Shook out my canvas free
> And like a pirate burst
>   Into that dreaming sea,
> The land knew no such thirst
>   As then tormented me.
>
> Now when at eve returned
>   I near that shore divine,
> Where once but watch-fires burned
>   I see thy beacon shine,
> And know the land hath learned
>   Desire that welcomes mine.   ('The Viking's Song', lines 1–12)

Kingsley Amis included this poem in his *Amis Anthology*, noting that 'Anyone who thinks that writing about physical sex cannot be genuine or natural unless it is "explicit" should consider this poem. The metaphor conveys much more – more tenderness and respect, for instance – than any imaginable direct statement could have done' (Amis, 1988: 335). The whole poem is indeed sexually charged – although only in the way that Dylan Thomas' 'If I Were Tickled by the Rub of Love', from a later

INTRODUCTION

period, is erotic – and Newbolt's nautical imagery is here used quite ingeniously to a very different and quite striking effect. In the same anthology Amis also included 'Ireland, Ireland', which was as close as Newbolt got to a political poem, with a tenor once again quite distant from his previous patriotic pieces: 'Ireland may be sad, wailing, and even unbalanced with grief, the poem suggests, but no false conciliation from, no alliance with, England can be seen as either acceptable or healing. The damage is irrevocable. And so this brief poem leaves us synchronously with a sharp and immutable political message, and the shifting, haunting image of Ireland herself' (Jackson, 1994: 119).

Such declamations, though, were now the exception rather than the rule; the political and public voices were gradually in retreat and, in *Songs of Memory and Hope* (1909) especially, Newbolt's poetry came as close to mimicking those he most admired (Hardy and Bridges) than it ever had before. This newly found maturity was best captured in two exquisite lyrics, 'Almore Altiero' and 'The Presentation', both of which elaborated a fully realized, adult conception of love, one which appeared rooted in his own unorthodox living arrangements: 'thou and I have wandered from the highway/ And found with hearts reborn/ This swift and unimaginable byway/ Unto the hills of morn' ('Almore Altiero', lines 1–4). In essence, Newbolt recognizes here that through trust and honesty, physical rivalries and jealousies of the sort which bedevil many conventional unions can be abandoned and his relationship with his wife can thereby exist on a higher plane, one in which either love displayed solely for selfish reasons or the withholding of sexual desire are no longer necessary. Rather, his wife's 'queenly pleasure' (her honest demands) are to be matched by Newbolt's 'golden treasure', which is his reverence for what she with love and truth will allow him to receive. A balance between give and take, acceptance and abeyance.

Paired with this, 'The Presentation' also reflects this philosophy in arguing that new life, here referring to Newbolt's son, is as much a product of two conjoined souls as it is of two bodies whose love has created that life. In Newbolt's mind, the basis for living in such a way meant an absolute equality of those souls, a point he advances here by turning on its head the traditional view of gender roles – 'The greater gives, the lesser doth conceive' ('The Presentation, line 16) – by acknowledging that the woman, in presenting him with the child (a product in both senses of the seed of his love) is now the greater of the two. Accepted male dominance thus becomes unconventional supplication. There is something vaguely Gravesian in the way in which

Newbolt consciously attempted to justify this part of his life and give a spiritual veneer to what was essentially a situation deriving from and driven by his own physical needs. Such a point was not lost on the book's reviewers, some of whom were able to recognize the subtle transformations taking place in his verse. In a lengthy review comparing Newbolt's book to new volumes by Alfred Noyes and William Watson, for example, the distinguished critic Percy Lubbock made a point of emphasizing this new direction, which was in contrast to those of his peers who had pointedly failed to adapt their style: 'The spirit which informs it [*Songs of Memory and Hope*] is genial and mellow, but has nothing to do with the relapse into comfortable beaming placidity which is the traditional farewell to youth of easy temperaments. It is still a spirit of adventure, but its raptures have become subtly intellectualized. Emotion has changed, has become less obvious, choicer, more intricate, but it has not lost romance' (Lubbock in *The Times Literary Supplement*, 18 November 1909: 437).

Being able to justify and philosophize to himself the complexities of his emotional life undoubtedly placed Newbolt on a more settled footing. This was not always to everyone's satisfaction with both Margaret and Ella taking umbrage at his new infatuation with Alice Hylton, wife of the 3rd Baron Hylton and daughter of the 3rd Marquess of Bristol. Newbolt's affair meant an outpouring of love poems and both he and Alice worked together on *The Book of Cupid* (1909), an anthology to which she provided the illustrations. Whatever the extent of their relationship – although they continued to correspond until his death – Newbolt at least found his own stability in confusion and turmoil. In addition, the increasing use he was making of Orchardleigh Park and the succour provided by its beautiful surrounds was another factor that perhaps accounted for the lighter tenor within some of his new poetry. In 1909 he published, under the name of Henry Nemo, *Goodchild's Garland*, a book of children's verses which captured the irreverence and whimsical surrealism so common to the youthful imagination. Just after that, and therefore too late to appear in the *Garland*, Newbolt wrote his most famous children's poem, 'Rilloby-Rill', whose quirky image of the grasshopper with a fiddle sounded the 'magic of its fairy music' (Kernahan, 1922: 105) and provided echoes of Walter de la Mare, another of his kindred poetic spirits. Aside from the lighter children's verses, 'Byron de Nos Jours' and 'An Essay on Criticism' even found Newbolt indulging in gentle satire, although with just enough added bite to make us wish their author had experimented further in that style.

INTRODUCTION

The latter in particular took Kipling to task over his recently published poem 'The Islanders', which had seen him turning on the very people he had previously sought to trumpet by condemning the working man's obsession with celebrity and organized games – 'the flannelled fools at the wicket or the muddied oafs at the goals' – at the expense of greater national priorities, in particular the threat posed by Germany and the need for national service. Having previously pointed out in an earlier essay Kipling's 'obvious misstatements and false statements' (Newbolt, 1902b: 1), Newbolt now set about offering a convincing parody of his particular style:

> ["]You shoot the pheasant, but it costs too much
> And does not tend to decimate the Dutch;
> Your duty plainly then before you stands,
> Conscription is the law for seagirt lands;
> Prate not of freedom! Since I learned to shoot
> I itch to use my ammunition boot."
>
> An odd way this, we thought, to criticize—
> This barrackyard "Attention! d— your eyes!"
> ('An Essay on Criticism', lines 79–85)

Best perhaps of all is 'Fidele's Grassy Tomb' which, although written a few years before, captures to greatest effect this often-overlooked lighter side to Newbolt. According to Michael McGarvie (1999) Newbolt's tale was inspired by a talk given to the Somerset Archaeological Society by Rev. J.B. Medley, which he had heard when making one of his periodic visits to Orchardleigh. According to local legend, a skeleton found in the recently excavated church was reputed to be that of a large dog who had saved a member of the local Champney family from drowning. As a show of thanks, the dog was commemorated in the park and, although the stone was destroyed, the only word it bore had been 'Fidele'. As McGarvie narrates, 'It was said that a former bishop ordered the body of the dog to be exhumed and buried elsewhere; but as the skull and skeleton of the animal were found in the church, the order must have been disobeyed and the monument erected as a blind' (McGarvie, 1999: 25). In Newbolt's retelling of the tale, it is the methodical sexton who, reflecting on the bishop's instruction, decides to take matters into his own hands: 'The grave was dug; the mason came/And carved on stone Fidele's name;/ But the dog that the Sexton laid inside/ Was a dog that never had lived or died' ('Fidele's Grassy Tomb', lines 45–48). The end of the poem brings the story up to date with the finding of the bones as well as providing a sly dig at the fastidious man of God. Not only is this ballad told in the best rollicking tradition but its light touch also belies the fact that loyalty was one of the key attributes Newbolt ascribed to the living of a moral life, associated as it was with ancient forms of allegiance and brotherhood. It can hardly have escaped Newbolt's notice that the name Fidele was so similar to the word fidelity and all that is associated with that particular virtue. Whatever the truth behind the story, the dog, whose loyalty was clearly shown both in the rescue of his master but also by his dying of sadness at the funeral, embodies the sort of life to be admired and emulated, lived as it was in pursuit of a higher ideal.

Verses such as these were, then, indicative of Newbolt's maturation as a writer and, although his poetry no longer sold in the numbers of years gone by, it had undoubtedly become more multi-faceted, deeper as well as more humorous, and, with modernism still embryonic, his was a reputation that continued to carry weight. This status as something of a Grand Old Man of English Poetry (although he was still only fifty in 1912!) was reflected in his election to the Athenaeum Club as well as in the part he played in professionalizing the British Academy. He became their inaugural Professor of Poetry and delivered a series of lectures, reported in *The Times*, in which he made a point of focusing on the Georgian poets who had only recently been published. Personally too, although saddened by the death of Dorothy, the wife of Lord Grey, who had become a close friend, and then angered by the more radical direction of the Liberal Party, Newbolt experienced happy times with the marriage on 2 June 1914 of his daughter Celia, who soon fell pregnant. In the same month as this welcome news was announced, however, Germany invaded Belgium. Little was Newbolt to envisage in that last long summer the role which the next few years were to play in his own reinvention and eventual decline.

The First World War and the End of the Ideal

Whilst it would be an exaggeration to claim that Newbolt foresaw the immediate causes of the First World War, his autobiography nonetheless indicated that he was all too aware of the shadows that could be seen to be lengthening inexorably across the continent: '1913 and 1914 were in this sense an overture ... almost every event and every scene of our ordinary life stood out with a peculiar vividness or a peculiar significance; they seem to have been purposely thrown upon the screen of our field of vision to show us by ironical contrast what a rich and settled life it was that we were called upon to stake so desperately' (Margaret Newbolt, 1942: 170). Nor was such a lament convenient hindsight after the fact; although his journalism may have been, for the most part, behind him, he maintained a keen interest in politics and he could count amongst his closest friends the Foreign Secretary Sir Edward Gray, the Secretary of State for War Richard Haldane as well as a number of senior military men including Field Marshal Douglas Haig. Newbolt was therefore more aware than most of the increasingly unstable, shifting, and fragile geopolitical situation. Something of this prevailing state of tension was captured in a short sequence entitled 'Songs of the Fleet', written following an invitation by Admiral Sir Reginald Custance in 1908 to observe at first hand the manoeuvres of the Channel Fleet. Kenneth Millard has made the point that, for all his tub-thumping qualities, 'many of his [Newbolt's] poems elaborate the theme of not knowing, and of not being able to know' (Millard, 1991: 34) and nowhere was that feeling better articulated than within these six fine poems. 'The Middle Watch', for instance, whose sombre tone reflects 'the beauty and the limitlessness of the sea' (Ibid., 35), seemed to offer little by way of comfort for the sailor seeking earthly reassurances: 'From a dim West to a dark East/ Our lines unwavering head,/ As if their motion long had ceased/ And Time itself were dead' ('The Middle Watch', lines 15–18). A later poem from the series proffered an even more explicit portent: 'What pulse of fear/ Beats with tremendous boom?' ('The Songs of the Guns at Sea', lines 4–5). In juxtaposing the implicit and barely heard ('pulse' suggests this) with more obvious clamours of noise, Newbolt was intimating the possibility of something cataclysmic building from silent and unexpected beginnings: 'Some day we're bound to sight the enemy,/ He's coming, tho' he hasn't yet a name' ('The Little Admiral', lines 28–29).

When such tensions did finally release in 1914, Newbolt could hardly be accused, therefore, of being caught off guard and, typically, his understanding of the unfolding events was informed by his views around gentlemanly fair play and the chivalric code. As we have seen, he had been formulating such ideas since his days at Oxford, extolling them in key poems, and had used these precepts to latterly argue that the way to maintaining peace lay in a 'Universal Association' in which member states were 'bound to one another in all circumstances by the obligation of brotherhood' and to only 'fight in a just quarrel and no other' (Newbolt, 1901: 9). Current events left little room for ambiguity; this was no such just quarrel, and Germany was seen to have broken the accepted rules of the game through her invasion of Belgium and subsequent sinking of the *Lusitania*. A war to stop her territorial ambitions, whilst regrettable for any loss of life, was, in this instance, wholly justified. On the day that the German Empire declared war on Russia, an unguarded Newbolt laid bare his immediate thoughts in no uncertain terms: 'the Germans stand for no civilising idea, but only for brute force in international life: to stand by and see them conquer France would be to watch the extermination of the most civilised by the most barbarous, and the establishment of blood and iron as the only right in the world' (Newbolt, letter to Alice Hylton, 1 August 1914, quoted in Margaret Newbolt, 1942: 189).

Newbolt was not of course alone amongst the intelligentsia in being unequivocal in his condemnation of the enemy. Kipling, for example, completely in character, was to warn that 'The Hun is at the Gate!' ('For All We Have And Are', line 4) and, as the war wore on, 'his hatred of Germans became obsessional' (Lycett, 2015: 641). Even the usually more placid Walter de la Mare could see that this was a period in which 'Idealism, nobility, romance' (Whistler, 1993: 233) risked being lost irrevocably. More subtly, the noted school inspector and poet Edmond Holmes believed that the origins of Germanic aggression could be found within their flawed system of schooling and its tendency toward docility, such that 'unquestioning obedience is the first of civic duties and the highest form of patriotism' (Holmes, 1916: 71). Newbolt's critique, although equally condemnatory, was however conceived under a quite different aspect, notably that the absence of decency in the conduct of German international affairs was indicative of a lack of national honour and any understanding of the rules governing fair play. In the end, war could only be considered just if it was undertaken both in and with the sort of spirit that pervaded the sports fields of the public schools where enemies were opponents and the rules of engagement were fully adhered to. As he had earlier written:

> To honour, while you strike him down,
> > The foe that comes with fearless eyes;
> To count the life of battle good,
> > And dear the land that gave you birth,
> And dearer yet the brotherhood
> > That binds the brave of all the earth— ('Clifton Chapel', lines 11–16)

INTRODUCTION

What Newbolt observed in the conduct of the Central Powers was, therefore, the greatest possible violation of these principles and, although at fifty-two too old to tilt his own lance, he was understandably keen to put his still-prodigious energies to use in the wider war effort. An established literary reputation, as well as his well-known Liberal leanings, meant that he was a natural choice to be amongst the Department of Information's writers tasked by C.F.G. Masterman with creating literature that would inspire and uphold the British cause. Eager to oblige, Newbolt embarked on a lecture tour across England putting forth his views on 'Patriotism and Poetry' whilst he also started work on a long running series of adventure stories for boys. These began with *The Book of the Blue Sea* (1914) and culminated in *The Book of the Grenvilles* seven years later. In addition, he found time to pen a history of the Oxfordshire and Buckinghamshire Light Infantry, the regiment of his son, Francis. By 1917, with a new Prime Minister (Lloyd George) and the country in need of invigoration, Newbolt was moved to the Intelligence Department of the Admiralty with a brief to serve up propaganda in support of the Royal Navy. His first commission, *Submarine and Anti-Submarine* (1918), was an account of the U-Boat conflict and later works included an official history of the navy's wartime activities. Research for these books took time and involved sifting through the many thousands of cables and communiqués sent to and from the Admiralty. Although beset with a crippling workload – he also chaired various committees connected to his intelligence role – he stuck diligently to his task. As Walter de la Mare later recalled, 'Throughout the War, however dark the day and louring the prospect, he [Newbolt] remained a steadfast optimist. He refused the easy refuge of despair, either on behalf of his own country, of the causes he had at heart, or of others in adversity. And if England was not inscribed upon his heart, then the scroll was blank' (de la Mare, 1939: vii).

For Newbolt, undertaking such demanding work was not only a way of assisting in defeating the hated Germans, and writing the history of the victor in the process, but, at a broader level, a means of fulfilling the expectations of the poet in times of crisis – one whereby he, unlike Yeats, could set the statesmen right. The state of his mind in this regard can easily be guessed at by a game he confessed to playing in which he imagined the role played in the war by his forebears. In his scheme, 'Shelley was a Consc. Objector but afterwards got a Commission in the Flying Corps ... Dr Johnson had a high position on the Press Bureau ... Sir Philip Sidney was in the Guards and got a posthumous V.C. ... Browning was a despatch rider' (Newbolt, letter to Alice

Hylton, 1 October 1916, quoted in Margaret Newbolt, 1942: 231–232). Newbolt likewise claimed to be 'mad with envy' at seeing photographs of Laurence Binyon carrying wounded soldiers on stretchers following the Battle of Verdun (Ibid., 227). Tasteless as such a claim may strike us today, this was not meant to be callous but simply an expression of the frustration Newbolt felt at not being able to 'play the game' and in this he was hardly alone. For him this must have been especially galling given the emergence of a new breed of Newboltian hero with those such as Custance, Jellicoe, Beatty, Haig, and Fisher inheriting the torch passed down from their celebrated predecessors. Many of these sentiments were to be articulated by Newbolt in a substantial prose work, *The Book of the Happy Warrior* (1917), which climaxed with the summoning of his countrymen to join 'this school for Happy Warriors' so as to be trained to fight the 'wild beasts, savages, maniacs, autocrats and worshippers of Woden' (Newbolt, 1917: 283). The vitriol aimed here at Germany was clear, and parts of *Happy Warrior* undoubtedly represented Newbolt at his worst when, momentarily carried away with nationalist zeal and sounding increasingly hot-blooded, he risked spilling over into xenophobia and racialism. Cecil Eby, for one, has condemned the book in no uncertain terms: 'Whether ... written out of sheer ignorance or with malice of afterthought, it is nonetheless an unconscionably jingoist book designed to wrench history into the service of recruiting fresh fodder for the guns of the Western Front' (Eby, 1987: 105).

However, laying to one side Newbolt's patriotic feelings and the manner in which they were on occasion expressed, and notwithstanding those aforementioned works commissioned by the government, it is to the *poetry* produced during this time that we should turn to in order to glean the most fulsome insights into his thinking. Although his output of new poems had slowed rapidly in the preceding years (no more than a dozen from 1909 to 1914) he was nonetheless inspired by the propaganda of the early months of the war and the call for the sort of writing that he could produce so well. In this he was not alone; Thomas Hardy's swaggering 'Men who March Away' and Rupert Brooke's sonnet 'Peace' stood out amongst the glut of flag-waving poems, not only as fine works in themselves, but also in putting forth the view that war, and this one in particular, was akin to a crusade. Often such a crusade, as Elizabeth Vandiver (2013) has demonstrated, was given an Hellenic aspect gleaned from a public school education – it was no coincidence that Brooke christened his unit sailing to Greece 'the Argonauts', whilst his friend and fellow traveller Patrick Shaw-Stewart produced the memorable poem

INTRODUCTION

'Achilles in the Trench'. Although rooted in different points of origin the parallels here with Newbolt's medieval chivalry are too strong to ignore, and should prompt us to remember that his views, far from being a hangover of Victorianism, were held, after a fashion, by several of the younger poets making their name in verse. In that manner, and drawing heavily on the idea of virtue being passed from one generation to the next, 'Hic Jacet' served as a stirring call to arms: 'To hear the heathen sweeping/ Over the lands he won;/ For he has left in keeping/ His sword unto his son' (lines 9–12). Similar was his urging of a grieving mother to remember that the sacrifice of her dead son was for a noble ideal: 'To keep the house unharmed/ Their fathers built so fair,/ Deeming endurance armed/ Better than brute despair' ('Farewell', lines 7–10).

These early years of the war also found Newbolt back in more familiar ballad territory. A case in point was 'The Toy Band', a poem recalling an incident involving Major General Sir Tom Bridges, the nephew of his old friend Robert, at St. Quentin on 27 August 1914, in which a retreating and bedraggled battalion are summoned back to fight by the discovery of a toy drum and penny whistle:

> "Rubadub! Rubadub! Wake and take the road again,
>   Wheedle-deedle-deedle-dee, Come, boys, come!
> You that mean to fight it out, wake and take your load again,
>   Fall in! Fall in! Follow the fife and drum!"
>   ('The Toy Band', lines 13–16)

Although only Newbolt could have made a retreat sound like a victory parade, this rollicking piece, the rhythms of which mirror the soldiers' marching boots, ranks among his best: 'it beats the road to Paradise (the paradise of hope and courage) as well as Valhalla' (Palmer, 1938: 44). Thus the younger Bridges, too, was destined to enter Newbolt's gallery of the great. Equally powerful was 'A Chanty of the Emden', another ballad-type poem which told of the destruction of the German raider SMS *Emden* by HMS *Sydney* at the Battle of Cocos in 1914:

> The *Sydney* she was straddled,
>   But the *Emden* she was strafed,
> They knocked her guns and funnels out,
>   They fired her fore and aft:
> They fired her fore and aft, my lads,
>   And while the beggar burned
> They salved her crew to a tune they knew,
>   But never had rightly learned— ('A Chanty of the Emden', lines 61–68)

Other poems in this manner included 'A Ballad of Sir Pertab Singh' – who commanded regiments in France at the age of seventy! – and 'The Service', a lengthy eulogy for his beloved Royal Navy (neither of which are included here). Newbolt may have been slightly out of step in assuming the navy would be the linchpin in any future conflict, but his sentiments as ever ring true, and there were few other contemporary poetic mentions of Jutland, in which here, 'Beatty raging with a lion's might/ roars out his heart to keep the foe from flight' (The Service', lines 75–76).

Alongside these new works went a reissuing of some of his earlier poems, although now the message and meaning had undergone a subtle shift. An example of this is to be found in 'The Invasion', written fifteen years previously, which on the surface documented the changing of the seasons with Winter seen as 'invading' the land prior to the rebirth of Spring:

So we wait the deliverer;
    Surely soon shall he come,
      Soon shall his hour be due:
Spring shall come with his greenery,
    Life be lovely again,
      Earth be the home we knew.   ('The Invasion', lines 25–30)

When originally published, these words were likely to have been read literally, with only the vaguest suggestion of a political message. Now, however, with an actual adversary looming large, they implied a meaning altogether more sinister; Germany may not have been planning for an invasion but she offered, like the hardening winter, a threat to the national way of life: 'Folk in thrall to the enemy,/ Vanquished, tilling a soil/ Hateful and hostile grown' (Ibid., lines 19–21). It is surely a testament to the universal and declarative power of Newbolt that lines such as 'England! wilt thou dare to-night/ Pray that God defend the Right?' ('The Vigil', lines 23–24) still spoke for the mood of the nation when it was reproduced in *The Times* in August 1914.

A consequence of his work re-entering the public domain in this way was that Newbolt's collected *Poems New and Old* went through five new editions whilst magazines and newspapers also clamoured to give space for reprints of his best-known verses. John Press (1971) has gone as far as to estimate that Newbolt sold over 70,000 copies of his books in the early years of the war whilst John Betjeman's judgement that 'even the most unliterary of chain bookshops [were] not afraid to stock them'

(Betjeman, 1940: xi) could not have been more true than at this time. Perhaps sensing the opportunity for sales, one magazine even devoted a five-page illustrated feature to Newbolt concluding that 'He has written much of which every Englishman may be proud – so have others; but mark the difference: he has written nothing of which the countrymen of Sidney, Nelson and Gordon need be ashamed' (*The Bookman*, November 1914: 39).

This unexpected second wave of popularity was, however, a consequence of the appetite for the types of poems that Newbolt was increasingly coming to see as a millstone around both his neck and pen. We have noted above the shift in tenor in his third and fourth volumes towards less effusive and more elegiac forms of commemoration and this shift was to be similarly replicated in the verses he produced during the period of the Great War. As Patric Dickinson has rightly observed, 'Newbolt was a complex personality: he had been for some time before 1914 dissatisfied with his style and had been meditating how to change it … . He knew what would be expected of him. Perhaps the way to 'do' the war, he thought, was ballads, but he no longer wanted to write ballads' (Dickinson, 1981: 23). Something of this desire for reinvention is captured in 'A Letter from the Front', which reads unlike anything Newbolt had previously written or was (more's the pity) ever to again. A free-verse digression on a fleeting morning incident involving an officer out hunting for a sparrow to feed his cat, the poem's content and form are a reminder of not just the whimsical side of Newbolt but also his too-often forgotten connections to the avant-garde. Indeed, there is, to these eyes at least, something of the spirit of Harold Monro in the conversational approach (as well as the cat!) and this link can be further solidified when one remembers that it was Newbolt who had been asked to open Monro's Poetry Bookshop in 1913 and he was to remain an advocate, even during these difficult years, for many emerging poets – even those who may not have shared his wider social outlook.

Any creative tensions felt by Newbolt were exacerbated by the toll the war was having on his personal life. Not only was he finding his tales for boys a 'poor substitute both for the poetry and novels that he wished to write, and for the harsh reality of the present war' (Jackson, 1994: 158) but familial anxieties too were weighing upon him. His son Francis and son-in-law Ralph Furse had enlisted early on, the former as a second lieutenant in the Oxford and Buckinghamshire Light Infantry and Ralph as a captain in the King Edward's Horse cavalry regiment. Both were soon called to the front, events which Newbolt described as leaving him with 'the feeling of one bruised head to foot' (Newbolt, letter to Alice Hylton, 4 April 1915, quoted in Margaret Newbolt, 1942: 203). Francis was to be invalided home after being badly injured at the Second Battle of Ypres and was to suffer recurrent bouts of shell-shock thereafter. Given his wide circle of friends and acquaintances such events were to be a regular topic of discussion within Newbolt's voluminous correspondence and it is revealing that his response, as we shall see later, was to seek retreat from the world, whether that was through extended stays at Netherhampton (his Wiltshire home) or in the imagination – his fantasy novel *Aladore* was written and published throughout the latter part of 1914.

Such retreats, however, were only temporary digressions and the business of churning out Boy's Own propaganda allowed little public opportunity for the expression of these intimate thoughts. It was, therefore, as so often, *poetry* which provided more private spaces with something of Newbolt's changing feelings being captured in the finest of his war poems, 'The War Films', part of whose unique nature stems from its inspiration being derived from actual televised footage of the war, in this instance Geoffrey Malins' popular documentary on the Battle of the Somme. The sense of the poem being a lament is apparent from the outset with the repetition of the quasi-liturgical 'O', although this was not simply to be a requiem for the sacrifice and heroism shown by the on-screen soldiers. Rather, it served as a threnody for the failure of orthodox religion, as well as its adherents, to truly comprehend the nature of sacrifice which Newbolt suggests here is akin to that of Christ – 'the faith we had not found' ('The War Films', line 6). There arises an interesting juxtaposition, therefore, in that a very modern, cutting-edge medium, notably film and cinema, is seen as providing insights into the most ancient of extant religious creeds, both High and Low Anglicanism – transcendent God in a 'cloudy Heaven' or imminent God 'on earth' – but also Catholicism ('seven sins and his sorrows seven' refers to the life of Mary). Such creeds have, according to Newbolt, functioned as a 'ragged cloak' in that they have obscured 'the secret of his birth' which can be taken to mean the true divinity of Christ embodied in his sacrifice on the cross, a sacrifice that is here mirrored by the actions of the soldiers. Film, on this occasion, allows us to bear direct witness. The final stanza sees Newbolt, in a quieter timbre, lamenting his inability to make such a sacrifice alongside the men, which parallels his earlier lament for the loss of the true meaning of Christ's divinity.

Outwardly straightforward, this is a more complex poem than may at first glance appear and raises wider questions, in its 18 lines, around not simply the specific sacrifice being made by the young men on screen (many whom would probably have been dead by the time the film was screened) but also the nature of sacrifice more generally as it linked to wider notions of faith. From his days at Clifton and the sermons of John Percival, Newbolt's had been a relatively straightforward, muscular sort of Christianity. However, the idea of a just war being fought in the manner of a crusade, an idea, as we have seen, popular early on in the war and driven in part by the renewed popularity afforded to his own work, was gradually being eroded from underneath him, a consequence of the increasingly mechanized and brutal nature of the conflict: 'The belief in chivalry was still there, but it was a chivalry far from Will Threlfall pounding down the touch line with the rugger ball or Julian Grenfell rejoicing that he had been born "at just the right time". It was a chivalry that was based on the foot soldier rather than the knight' (Chitty, 1997: 249). Extending this point still further, Jan Morris (1978) has gone as far as to pinpoint this poem ('The War Films') as seminal in marking an epochal shift in our understanding of heroism. From now on, the imperial balladeers were to be muted and old shiny splendour was forever tarnished.

As with Owen, Sassoon and, most notably, Vera Brittain, whose respective faiths were called into question, we therefore see chinks emerging in Newbolt's orthodox armour. Although it might never have been fully breached it is nonetheless telling that his most heartfelt comment on the war was entitled 'A Perpetual Memory' and its four barbed lines summarized more of his feelings than any number of brow-beating ballads ever could:

> BROKEN and pierced, hung on the bitter wire,
>   By their most precious death the Sons of Man
> Redeem for us the life of our desire—
>   O Christ how often since the world began!
> ('A Perpetual Memory', lines 1–4)

These lines, written in the 1920s, are testament to the profound effect that this period had on Newbolt. Whilst never to experience this (or any) fighting directly, his vicarious involvement behind the lines allowed him to observe from distance an unravelling of many of the certainties and ideals he had long held dear and which had been the bedrock of his system of beliefs. The age of celebration, to which Newbolt was in part a chronicler, was over.

The Public Man in Later Life

The Great War had both (re-)made and yet also unmade Henry Newbolt. In the early months of the fighting his poetry had enjoyed something of a resurgence and he once again became the mouthpiece for a nation in need of a hefty dose of patriotism. That so many readers and soldiers could once again find solace in poems such as 'The Vigil' and, inevitably perhaps, 'Vitaï Lampada', only added weight to the view that these represented universal messages of heroism-in-verse. At a point in time when the nature of the conflict was being constructed in the image of the public schools – that is to say, a crusade against evil to be undertaken with an instinctive sense of fraternal duty – Newbolt's work, which spoke to a deeper philosophy of gallantry, sounded loudly. Its sentiments even resonated in a roundabout way with a younger generation of poets; what else, after all, was Julian Grenfell's comparison of war to a big picnic than a more up-to-date form of playing the game? New poems such as 'The Toy Band', 'A Chanty of the Emden' and 'The King's Highway' provided glimpses of the old strut and rivalled anything he had previously written. Wilfred Owen for one thought the latter was 'splendid!' (Owen, letter to Susan Owen, 18 August 1915, 355 in Owen, 1967: 355).

However, by 1916, with the war having long settled into its predictable attritive pattern, such views were coming to be seen as outdated. Lest we forget, many of Newbolt's patriotic pieces, which had been hastily reprinted and were so inspiring early on, were now nearly twenty years old and had been written with a very different set of circumstances in mind, at a time when the navy held sway and deeds of imagined derring-do in far-off lands were still (just) possible. Instead, this was a new world of total warfare, in which the trench line had replaced the cavalry charge, and tanks and machine guns had facilitated more brutal and mechanical ways of killing: 'The gamesmanship taught on the playing field proved to be an inadequate preparation for the pitiless dehumanization of modern warfare encountered on the Western Front' (Eby, 1987: 108). Newbolt thus perched awkwardly between the interstices of two hemispheres; a late Victorian amid an age of crashing modernity.

Whilst this characterization is accurate, it will not do to suggest that Newbolt was blind to or ignorant of the realities of what was taking place around him. He remained profoundly invested in the continuing conflict, both personally through his friends and relations at the front, but also professionally via his tireless work for various government departments which kept him abreast of the latest tactics and strategies.

INTRODUCTION

It was perhaps this knowledge which led him to the realization that his particular gifts for celebration and commemoration were no longer appropriate in capturing the experiences of the ordinary soldier. In commenting for example on Newbolt's patriotic ballads, Vanessa Jackson has rightly pointed out how 'he never attempted to render trench warfare (or any of the tragic second half of the war) in this form' (Jackson, 1994: 113) and it is unlikely anyway if such forms would by then – from 1916 onwards – have found much favour. Instead, a poem such as 'The War Films' (discussed above) suggested something of his true feelings and was all the stronger for this authenticity. Yet Newbolt still seemed unable or unwilling to fully cede to this impulse and he remained, as ever, a public poet yoked to his sense of duty. Even as late as 1918, his lengthy paean to the Royal Navy, 'The Service', was sold for £500 as part of *The Daily Telegraph*'s King George's Fund for Sailors (see *The Daily Telegraph*, 2 March 1918).

Nor was it simply that Newbolt had been overtaken by wider events not of his own making. There had always been, as has been suggested, an antediluvian part to his character and he was often suspicious of progress for its own sake, an aspect displayed in earlier essays in which he had not only extolled the joys of fox hunting (see Newbolt, 1902c) but also showed a deep distrust of the motor car (see Newbolt, 1904)! His Liberalism, after all, had always been more about what was fair and right rather than what was possible. Now, however, he was having to come to terms with an age that had not only revealed its ugliness through new forms of warfare but which had also, in the process, shown itself as totally antithetical to his entire world view. Crusade had become sacrifice; chivalry had become survival. Film – another aspect of modernity and therefore an article of potential suspicion – had stripped away the mystique surrounding the deeds of the hero and the heroic. Newbolt, and those of the imperial generation, were neither able nor fit to speak of them: 'The disillusioned soldiers who returned ... were weary of martial ardours, weary of patriotism, weary of any kind of emotionalism' (Palmer, 1938: 43). Such an epochal shift was clear from the lukewarm reception afforded to *St. George's Day* (1918); it was barely reviewed and emerged almost as an afterthought at the tail end of the war.

The last two decades of Newbolt's life were then to be marked by an absence of new poetry, a fact remarked upon by Padric Dickinson: 'as *Admirals All* had changed his course from being only a poet to being a man of letters and affairs, so the war inevitably took him further away'

(Dickinson, 1981: 24). There was still the series of adventure stories for boys to finish and in 1920 he also brought out his own account of the navy during the war. Later, the last two authorized volumes of the official naval history of the war (1928 and 1931) were given to Newbolt to complete when the historian Julian Corbett died before it could be finished. By this stage he had become a fully-fledged establishment and Whitehall man with a reputation which meant that 'He [now] moved in the highest social circles, being frequently invited to dine both at the Palace and at Mansion House, and to share boxes at the opera with persons of importance' (Chitty, 1997: 269). In 1922 he was made a Companion of Honour to add to his earlier knighthood. A year later he embarked on a long lecture tour in Canada as a guest of the Canadian Council, and he was regularly asked to sit on public boards and committees.

Whilst many of these were uninspiring affairs with no legacy to speak of, his work in education is worthy of further mention not least as its impact continued to be felt late into the century. As chairman of a Departmental Committee for the Board of Education, it was Newbolt who was to write much of its subsequent report, *The Teaching of English in England*, often referred to simply as 'the Newbolt Report'. Although some such as Stefan Collini have argued that the eponymous report was 'marked by a tone of robust jingoism' (Collini, 1991: 366), in recent years historians of education have offered more sophisticated interpretations, rightly preferring to see it as a seminal and forward-looking document, especially in its anticipation of later curricular initiatives such as the introduction of compulsory citizenship lessons in schools. As Brenton Doecke summarizes, 'The Report presents an argument for educational reform, including a case for the centrality of the literary imagination to any education that is worthy of the name' (Doecke, 2017: 436). Deploying language which speaks uncannily to many of the concerns of our own time, the report further pointed to 'the danger that a true instinct for humanism may be smothered by the demand for definite measurable results, especially the passing of examinations' ('Newbolt Report', 1921: 55) and that a greater clarity on the agreed purposes of education as a whole meant more opportunities to 'bridge the social chasms which divide us' (Ibid., 6). In light of such claims, John Perry is right to point out that 'The report [sic] was clearly motivated in part by a belief in social justice, rather than by a focus on performativity' (Perry, 2019: 242) and this motivation originated from the diverse approaches to learning that its authors saw as necessary in order to pique children's interest. Newbolt for one was not blind to the fact that there were many ways in which the imagination could be stimulated and the report's discussion of individual lessons was to stress that 'We do not suggest that only the recognised English classics should be included ... the teacher who means the effect of his work to be lasting will start from what the children themselves enjoy' ('Newbolt Report', 1921: 84).

This belief that the most effective form of education was that which drew upon the child's instinctive interests not only had its roots in earlier Romanticism, going back to Rousseau's *Emile*, but was also an important plank of the sorts of progressive thinking that were to be regularly revisited later on in the century, most famously within the child-centred Plowden Report of 1967. In becoming a well-known champion of such methods, it was therefore unsurprising that Newbolt was asked to give the opening address to the 1922 conference of the New Ideals in Education group, a loose alliance of progressive educators, policy makers, and radicals, all of whom were looking for alternative models to traditional schooling. That the archetypal public-school poet could happily promote experiential learning alongside the firebrand A.S. Neill (founder of Summerhill, the infamous 'school without rules') as well as the mystical Victor Bulwer-Lytton, 2nd Lord Lytton, is testament to the malleability of Newbolt's mind and his openness to new ideas. It would surely have been easy for him to advocate for the continuation of more didactic forms of learning that had formed so much a part of his own boyhood.

Alongside the report's call for the content of lessons to appeal directly to the needs of the child – and through his own production of adventure stories for boys we cannot doubt that Newbolt saw the validity of cheaper fiction and its place in schools – went similar appeals for literature to reinforce a sense of social cohesion by drawing upon a collective national culture. In citing the example of France, the report made the point that, 'It [literature] is considered not only as a means of developing the power of expression, both oral and written, by giving the child a thorough knowledge of the structure of the language, but it is looked upon also as an instrument of national culture and moral education' (Ibid., 369). In this there was clearly something of the spirit of Matthew Arnold, who had previously argued for the importance of schools in acting to unify and break down the class barriers within society. Education, broadly understood, and the creation of what today would be referred to as a sense of 'identity' were, therefore, to be an important aspect of Newbolt's post-war thinking, one which spilled over into his other endeavours.

In 1921 he was appointed Editor-in-Chief of Nelson's Teaching of English series by John Buchan, whilst he also set about compiling *An English Anthology of Prose and Poetry* in 1921, *The Tide of Time in English Poetry* in 1925, and *New Paths on Helicon* in 1927. Introductions to the great poets flowed and these were often intended for schoolchildren as much as for the general reader. Stultifying as the work no doubt was, it at least allowed Newbolt the consolation of bringing to a new readership the very best of the canon with the hope that knowledge of it stood to create a wider equality of opportunity, thereby neutering some of the advantages held by those with access to elite education. Taking over from Prime Minister Stanley Baldwin as President of the English Association in 1927, Newbolt, in a short pamphlet, reiterated these themes by calling both for education to be kept out of the hands of party politics (which would 'bring it death rather than life' (Newbolt, 1928: 10)) but also by stating that the organization which he now represented had an obligation to provide a 'lifelong course and unlimited freedom of entrance' (Ibid., 12) to the world of literature. Whilst we may now take issue with Newbolt's uncontested acceptance of an homogeneous national identity (although in his defence he was speaking well before the onset of mass immigration and multiculturalism), his desire to see literature used as a way to create greater equality of opportunity spoke powerfully to the liberal/Liberal part of his character, an aspect which could be traced back nearly forty years to his work in the East End of London and his observations of urban squalor. Straightforward as his interpretation of society may have been, Newbolt's view that literature had a value beyond that of being studied simply for its own sake and that it could be used as a means to ameliorate deeper social problems, echoes the sentiments of later educational theorists and makes more impressive any assessment of his achievements and character.

Throwing himself wholeheartedly into his educational work, as well as now being in high demand as a public speaker, meant, as has been previously suggested, that less time than ever was available for the production of verse. In any case, the prolific public poet of three decades earlier had long since disappeared, the chastening effect of the war having had a large part to play in that. Adding to the impression that these were fallow years was the fact that despite Newbolt's popular collected poems (*Poems: New and Old*) being reprinted almost annually up to 1928, the contents of its later editions remained unchanged. That being said, whilst he may only have been now a part-time poet, the few pieces he did produce in the twenties are intriguing for they witness

INTRODUCTION

the emergence of a more intimate voice free of his earlier triumphalist rhetoric. Whilst it would be stretching a point to say that this represented a 'second career' (Chitty, 1997: 264), and he was never quite able to develop as satisfactorily as he may have liked the flatter conversational approach of his friend Bridges, the poems from later in his life – which were posthumously collected and published as *A Perpetual Memory* (1939) – were nonetheless suggestive of a new direction, one in which time and the passing of time emerged as the dominant theme. It was hardly unusual of course for a poet to become more insular in his older age; however this development came at a point in Newbolt's life when, in common with other creative types, he was striving to come to terms with the sense of loss engendered by the war. This 'return to order' saw artists and writers falling back on traditional subject matter, often landscape, as a means to counter the horrors that modernity had unleashed. Although this was a movement most associated with the visual arts (see Chambers, 2018), something of this juxtaposition can be observed also in the work of Edmund Blunden, whose poetry of this time (*The Waggoner and Other Poems* was published in 1920) balanced the recollections of a war which he had observed directly with the ruralism of the Kentish countryside of his youth. Whilst Newbolt had been too old to have experienced at first hand any of the horrors depicted by those younger war poets, as one reared on past imperial glories his loss was all the more profound with the tenets he had long held dear – chivalry, nobility, fair play, and courage – having been thrown to the wolves amid the new and bloody modes of combat.

In response to this challenge, which given his age he was hardly now in a position to confront directly, Newbolt's world became correspondingly more intimate and parochial. Although remaining diligent toward his public obligations and committee work, the summer months found him spending more time than ever not just in Orchardleigh Park but also at his other retreat of Netherhampton House (leased from his in-laws) in Wiltshire, about two miles from Salisbury. With their country gardens, traceable histories, and space for contemplation, Newbolt's homes and surroundings were in step with his prevailing mood. Two poems from this time, amongst the finest and yet also most uncharacteristic things he wrote, were symbolic of this change. First, in May 1924 came 'The Linnet's Nest' in which, amid 'this cistus of delight,/ A mound of delicate pure white crinkled petals' (lines 9–10), the poet recalls finding the nest of a linnet who sits trembling to protect her eggs. Despite lacking 'That [what] we call knowledge, nor such love and hope as ours' (Ibid., line

22) its presence instigates a meditation not simply upon the fact that images of such beauty are sustained by virtue of their being able to be recollected but also that there is life beyond the mere mortal: 'To be one with that spirit from whom all life springs,/ And therein to behold all beauty for ever' (Ibid., lines 39–40). Although it would be tempting after that fashion to read the last stanza as a plea for Romantic pantheism as suggested by the linnet being 'a part of His immortal dream' (Ibid., line 43) the key to understanding the poem surely lies earlier on in reference to the 'vast eternal memory' (Ibid., line 36). This belief in an *anima mundi* was becoming of increasing interest to Newbolt, not perhaps as the gestalt collective memory of the sociologist Maurice Halbwachs, but rather in the Yeatsian appeal to tradition that the great Irishman had articulated in his meditations on Coole Park, another pseudo-aristocratic estate. As Yeats had used the house and its occupants (notably Lady Augusta Gregory) as a means to commune with the past so Newbolt, in a more microscopic way, here deployed the small picture of the linnet and her nest to indicate that the past in its images, its seasons, and its beauty will not die but persist into the present through such remembrance: 'in my mind their loveliness will still survive/ Till I too in my turn obey the laws of dust' (Ibid., lines 31–32). Both history and tradition, as forms of national inheritance, had long fascinated Newbolt; now however, filtered through the lens of the pastoral and the incidents of his immediate surroundings, it was being given a more philosophical and melancholy veneer.

On a similar theme to 'The Linnet's Nest' was 'The Nightjar', written exactly a year later in May 1925, in which the poet recounts his attempt to rescue and nurse back to health the eponymous creature. As in the previous instance, Newbolt here uses the image of the small bird to embody a wider truth – in this case that beauty can touch the soul yet must ultimately die with the passing of time: 'even now, like all beauty of earth,/ She is fading from me into the dusk of Time' ('The Nightjar', lines 20–21). Such loss was seen as emblematic of the dichotomy of 'Wonder and Reason' (Ibid., line 13) which, as Patric Dickinson has again observed, 'were the poles of his [Newbolt's] genius and personality' (Dickinson, 1981: 26). In the case of this particular poem, the Wonder of the 'soul's ocean cave' was to be apprehended through the Reason of the human body ('optic nerve') and its creations ('full fathom five', borrowed from Shakespeare, suggests man-made ships) ('The Nightjar', lines 12–13). Furthermore, the Wonder of the mystery being revealed is countered by the Reason of the flat, direct, and prosaic language by which it is

INTRODUCTION

expressed. In relation to Newbolt's broader outlook, the Wonder of chivalry, etiquette, and fraternal bondage had come up against the cold Reason of the real world and its forms of materialism and dishonour. The Wonder of an imagined, mythic past governed by agreed forms of virtue had met with full force the Reason of *realpolitik* and the conflicts it had wrought.

Such a conflict between these two poles had perhaps always been latent in his work and unreconciled; however, these last years saw it coming to the fore. It was to reach its apogee in 'The Star in the West', the final poem Newbolt was to write (although regrettably it was not placed last in *A Perpetual Memory*) and which was first published in the Christmas 1932 edition of *The Listener*. A visionary poem, and therefore again uncharacteristic, it found him meditating on the increasingly bleak political situation as another war with Germany began to seem a distinct possibility: 'That men have murdered Night, and made stars of their own,/ And flung them down from heav'n, and Peace has died by fire' ('The Star in the West', lines 15–16). A point of contrast can surely be drawn here with Kipling's 'The Storm Cone' (1936), which sounded comparable cautionary notes. While the latter saw fit to draw upon the image of a bereft ship and turbulent weather as a metaphor for the emerging threats to our way of life, so Newbolt preferred the symbol of an ancient star. This was telling; Newbolt had always been one to look to history as a means of informing action in the present, but here his gaze extended back further still, not simply through the object of the star which is seen by observers today as it looked thousands of years ago, thereby allowing us to glimpse something of our own origins, but also through his invocation of the nativity, a story forming the bedrock of our extant culture. Even in this, his only 'Thirties poem', Newbolt could not escape the pull of history and a thousand years of tradition, and whilst stylistically the piece is clearly anachronistic, being a world away from Auden and his followers, it is also timeless, tapping as it does into the long-shared myths of a common heritage. It therefore represents a fitting conclusion to his corpus of poetry, one of whose key threads had been a belief that history exists in the present and that it has lessons to teach us. By the time of publication of this sparkling coda, Newbolt may have wished we had paid closer heed.

Conclusion

The last years of Newbolt's life were far from happy. By 1934 he was showing signs of the disease which, although mysterious at the time to those around him, was latterly diagnosed as a form of Parkinson's. Although he never fully lost his memory or suffered any obvious cognitive decline, and he could still answer questions when prompted, his was to be a long retreat into himself to the point that he ultimately became completely withdrawn from his surroundings. Accompanying this went the loss of the ability and desire to write, correspond, and converse. Living arrangements at Orchardleigh and Netherhampton were by this stage clearly unsuitable and so the Newbolts took the decision to move in with Ella Coltman in London. Among other things this meant abandoning many of the thousands of books they had accumulated over the course of their long married life. Having shed so much of what had been dear to him, Newbolt eventually died on 19 April 1938. Vanessa Jackson recounts how after his death Margaret was to find a little piece of paper containing the Grace of his old Oxford College which he had read ritually to himself every night. As she elaborates, 'In withdrawing from the daily life around him, Newbolt had returned to a representation of sanity, of youth, of aspirations as yet unchecked by the paths he himself took, or by the drastic and unforeseen events that were to change the world in which he lived' (Jackson, 1994: 184). More than this, though, in finding solace in such an ancient tradition Newbolt was to the end both recognizing and embodying his part in the great national inheritance and the fact that this served to sustain him is not merely poignant but provides a fitting element of circularity to a life that had always looked to the past in order to offer hope for the future.

Newbolt's ashes were laid to rest at the small island church at Orchardleigh which had long been a burial place for members of the Duckworth family. When Margaret died in 1960 she was placed next to him. Today the house and its grounds have been turned into a wedding venue hotel and golf course, although it has, despite the commercialism, managed to retain something of the remote character which for many years so appealed to its most famous resident. Following his death, the tone of the tributes was respectful rather than effusive and tended to focus as much on his wider literary activities and educational work as on his poetry. An exception was the panegyric provided by Walter de la Mare for *The Times,* which spoke of Newbolt as being 'alert as a kestrel-like the figurehead on a vessel voyaging over seas which, however familiar they might be, might at any moment reveal the unforeseen and the strange. The intent grey-blue eyes pierced into ones own through a remote haze, as it were, of his mind's reverie' (de la Mare in *The Times*, 25 April 1938).

Respect there was but only in the way that the old are sometimes thanked for their service yet also gently pitied for being of the past. As a man whose reputation was made by one conflict and then brought down by another, it is likely that the Second World War, which started only in the year after his passing, would have been a fight too far for Newbolt and one that he may well have struggled to comprehend and capture in verse. He perhaps lacked the visionary talents of his old champion Laurence Binyon, whose meditative 'The Burning of the Leaves' (1942), written as a civilian, was a high watermark of the period, nor had he ever truly assimilated the versifying intellectualism of Eliot. Those chroniclers of the new heroism – younger men such as John Pudney and Roy Fuller – had not only first-hand understanding of the new modes of fighting but also a residual modernism which saved their poems from sounding anachronistic in a way that Newbolt's would surely have done. After 1945, wider and more rapid changes further accelerated the dismantling of much of the old world; the remnants of Britain's imperial control were ceded, her armed forces (especially the navy) were reduced in size, and the social graces and mores that defined the Edwardian era rapidly disappeared. Tradition was out and three decades after Newbolt's death – conceivably within a lifetime – his past looked like a foreign country.

Yet what do these facts matter? After all, recent reclamations of poets such as Walter de la Mare (Sweeney, 2006 and Wootten, 2021), W.E. Henley (Howlett, 2017), and Binyon himself (O'Prey, 2016) suggest that any academic consensus about the period has been far from reached and that even more obviously traditional, and in some cases unfashionable, writers still have a broad appeal for the scholar as much as the general reader. Even if that were not the case, recourse to a more contemporary lens still reveals much about the specific case of Newbolt to which we can be sympathetic. For one thing, his work was obviously democratic in that it was both accessible to, and able to be accessed by (through its publication in cheap newspapers), a wide readership. Previously, poetry had, more often than not, been the preserve of the middle classes; Newbolt as much as Kipling broke with that tradition by publishing verses which could be read and appreciated by people from all social backgrounds. How many other poets have had their poems emblazoned on newspaper placards as happened to Newbolt when, on the day of its publication, 'DRAKE'S DRUM' was to be found on every street corner as a form of promotional advertising for his latest offering (see Newbolt, 1932: 186)? Nor should it be forgotten that many of these bold and loud-sounding early poems were intentionally written with the casual reader in mind, free as they were from wider literary allusions and intellectual points of reference.

We should move too to adjusting our appreciation and understanding of the substance of these poems. The foolishness inherent in judging the moral and social standards of the past by those of the present has too often led to Newbolt's poetry being read under the assumption that it served as an apologia for the worst aspects of the nineteenth century. Approaching any poet already convinced as to the merits of their work is bad enough; it is worse, however, in the case of Newbolt as it has allowed for the persistence of abject falsehoods. That Newbolt believed in the importance of empire was certain; however, this was hardly uncommon at the time nor was his a vision in which subjugation or disadvantage had any part. If anything, his views prefigure that of the modern Commonwealth, and his thinking was never hierarchical. Furthermore, when we consider, at a broader level, Newbolt's patriotism, it is worth heeding the point made by J.H. Grainger that '[it] did something for the losers' (Grainger, 1986: 76), and Newbolt was always mindful of those in the world who may have needed forms of support. His vigorous championing of Liberal ideas is testament to that. Nor, for all his clamour to play the game, was he a believer in winners and losers; he believed firmly that if both sides played fairly and according to the rules of engagement, there was no shame in defeat, and the beaten were not to be condemned for having lost but rather applauded for their participation. Whilst the chivalric ideal – of which this view was a part – may now be unfashionable, this does not mean that it was ever 'wrong', and in modern-day sporting worship it perhaps finds an approximate equivalent.

The critic Jerome Buckley long ago attested to the fact that '[Newbolt] transcended the frantic bluster of the mere jingo' (Buckley, 1981: 227) and in so doing he offers us, through his poetry, a window on a period of transformation in British history as the certainties of the Victorian era, which included certainties around Britain's place and role in the world, extended into the Edwardian period and a new century. That this subsequent period was something of an Indian summer, in which new currents of ideological and creative thinking were merely being held at bay, is apparent when we witness the rapid and irreparable fracturing of society caused by the First World War. This total conflict brought to an end the Long Nineteenth Century and what were by now seen as out-of-date social structures. Socialism and Modernism emerged. In his more elegiac moods Newbolt was able to capture this end to Victorianism, the emergence of doubt (about religion, politics, and the old order) and, finally, the evaporation of a world he had long sought to chronicle. His loss of a poetic voice after 1918 is therefore suggestive of something lost that was bigger than one man. In his loss, however, he showed glimpses of what Britain had been and the beliefs which had driven her forward. He also added to the myth. That should be achievement enough.

Works Cited in the Introduction and Notes:

Works By Newbolt:
A Naval History of the War 1914–1918. London: Hodder and Stoughton, 1920.
A Perpetual Memory and Other Poems. London: John Murray, 1939.
Admirals All and Other Verses. Shilling Garland Series No. 8. London: Elkin Matthews, 1897.
Aladore. Edinburgh: Blackwood, 1914.
(As Editor) *An English Anthology of Prose and Poetry Showing the Main Stream of English Literature Through Six Centuries (14th Century–19th Century)* 2 vols. London: Dent, 1921.
'British Ballads' in *The English Review*, Vol. 21 (Dec. 1915), 452–470.
Goodchild's Garland: Diversions and Perversions. London: Elkin Mathews, 1909.
Mordred: A Tragedy. London: Unwin, 1895.
'Motors and Manslaughter', *The Monthly Review*, Vol. 16 (Aug. 1904), 1–8.
My World as in My Time: Memoirs of Sir Henry Newbolt 1862–1932. London: Faber and Faber, 1932.
Naval Operations. Vol. 4. and Vol. 5. History of the Great War Based on Official Documents. London: Longmans, Green, 1928 and 1931.
(As Editor) *New Paths on Helicon.* London: T. Nelson & Sons, 1927.
Poems New and Old. London: John Murray, 1912.
'Public Schools and Their Critics', *The Monthly Review*, Vol. 8, Issue 24 (Sept. 1902a), 1–7.
Songs of Memory and Hope. London: John Murray, 1909.
'Sport and Cruelty', *The Monthly Review*, Vol. 7, Issue 19 (April 1902c), 1–9.
St. George's Day and Other Poems. London: John Murray, 1918.
Submarine and Anti-Submarine. London: Longmans, Green, 1918.

Taken from the Enemy. London: Chatto and Windus, 1892.
(As Editor) *The Book of Cupid, Being an Anthology from the English Poets*. London: Constable, 1909.
The Book of the Blue Sea. London: Longmans, Green, 1914.
The Book of the Grenvilles. London: Longmans, Green, 1921.
The Book of the Happy Warrior. London: Longmans, Green, 1917.
'The Happy Warrior', *The Monthly Review*, Vol. 2, Issue 5 (Feb. 1901), 1–10.
The Idea of an English Association. The English Association Pamphlet No. 70. Oxford: Oxford University Press, 1928.
The Island Race. London: Elkin Mathews, 1898.
'The Lordliest Life on Earth', *The Monthly Review*, Vol. 6, Issue 17 (Feb. 1902b), 1–6.
The Old Country: A Romance. London: Smith, Elder, 1906.
'The Paradox of Imperialism', *The Monthly Review*, Vol. 1, Issue 1 (Oct. 1900), 1–14.
The Sailing of the Long-Ships and Other Poems. London: John Murray, 1902.
(As Editor) *The Teaching of English in England* (also known as 'The Newbolt Report'). London: HMSO, 1921.
(As Editor) *The Tide of Time in English Poetry*. London and Edinburgh: Nelson, 1925.
The Twymans: A Tale of Youth. Edinburgh: Blackwood, 1911.

Works About Newbolt:
John Betjeman, 'Sir Henry Newbolt, C.H.', John Betjeman (Ed.), *Selected Poems of Henry Newbolt*. London: Thomas Nelson and Sons, 1940, ix–xv.
Michael Bright, 'Remembering Sir Henry Newbolt: An Essay and Bibliography', *English Literature in Transition, 1880–1920*, Vol. 33, No. 2 (1990), 155–178.
Susan Chitty, *Playing the Game: A Biography of Henry Newbolt*. London: Quartet Books, 1997.
Patric Dickinson, 'Henry Newbolt, 1862–1938', Patric Dickinson (Ed.), *Selected Poems of Henry Newbolt*. London: Hodder and Stoughton, 1981, 11–27.
Ralph Furse, 'Vitaï lampada tradidit', Henry Newbolt, *A Perpetual Memory and Other Poems*. London: Murray, 1939, ix–xvi.
David Gervais, 'Sir Henry John Newbolt (1862–1938), Poet and Writer', *Oxford Dictionary of National Biography*. Available online at: https://www.oxforddnb.com/view/10.1093/ref:odnb/9780198614128.001.0001/odnb-9780198614128-e-35212.
Vanessa Jackson, *The Poetry of Henry Newbolt: Patriotism is Not Enough*. Greensboro: ELT Press, 1994.
Walter de la Mare, 'Sir Henry Newbolt. Mr Walter de la Mare's Tribute', *The Times*, 25 April 1938.

INTRODUCTION

Walter de la Mare, 'Sir Henry Newbolt, C.H., 1862–1938', Henry Newbolt, *A Perpetual Memory and Other Poems*. London: Murray, 1939, v–viii.
Margaret Newbolt (Ed.), *The Later Life and Letters of Sir Henry Newbolt*. London: Faber, 1942.
Paul Webb, 'Newbolt for Poets' Corner', *The Spectator*, 19 December 1987, 54–55.
Derek Winterbottom, *Henry Newbolt and the Spirit of Clifton*. Bristol: Redcliffe, 1986.

Other Works Cited:
Kingsley Amis (Ed.), *The Amis Anthology*. London: Hutchinson, 1988.
Anon., 'Books of the Week. Recent Verse: Review of *Admirals All and other Verses*', *The Times*, 5 November 1897, 13.
Anon., 'Briefer Mention. Review of *Admirals All*', *The Academy*, 30 October 1897, 349.
Anon., 'Lyra Heroica: Review of *The Island Race*', *The Academy*, 3 December 1898, 371.
Anon., 'Recent Poetry and Verse: Review of *Admirals All*', *The Speaker*, 11 December 1897, 667–668.
Anon., 'Review of *Admirals All and other Verses*', *The Athenæum*, 22 January 1898, 111–112.
Anon., 'Review of The Old Country', *The Athenæum*, 8 December 1906, 730.
Anon., 'Some Recent Verse including *Clifton Chapel, and Other Poems*', *The Edinburgh Review*, October 1909, 378–399.
Anon., 'The Literary Week', *The Academy*, 16 December 1899, 711–714.
William Archer, *Poets of the Younger Generation*. London and New York: John Lane, The Bodley Head, 1902.
Edith Batho and Bonamy Dobrée, *The Victorians and After, 1830–1914*. London: Cresset, 1938.
Chris Brooks and Peter Faulkner, 'Introduction', Chris Brooks and Peter Faulkner (Eds.), *The White Man's Burdens: An Anthology of British Poetry of the Empire*. Exeter: University of Exeter Press, 1996, 1–50.
Robert Buchanan, 'Under the Beard of Buchanan', *Blackwood's Magazine*, February 1899, 264–271.
Jerome Buckley, *The Victorian Temper: A Study in Literary Culture*. Cambridge: Cambridge University Press, 1981.
Emma Chambers (Ed.), *Aftermath: Art in the Wake of World War One*. London: Tate Publishing, 2018.
Stefan Collini, *Public Moralists: Political Thought and Intellectual Life in Britain 1850–1930*. Oxford: Clarendon, 1991.
Cyril Connolly, *Enemies of Promise*. London: G. Routledge & Sons, 1938.
A.H. Cooper-Prichard, *Conversations with Oscar Wilde*. London: Philip Allan, 1931.

David Daiches, *Poetry and the Modern World: A Study of Poetry in England Between 1900 and 1939*. Chicago: University of Chicago Press, 1940.

Brendon Doecke, 'What Kind of "Knowledge" is English? (Re-reading The Newbolt Report)', *Changing English*, Vol. 24, No. 3. (2017), 230–245.

Cecil Eby, *The Road to Armageddon: The Martial Spirit in English Popular Literature, 1870–1914*. Durham: Duke University Press, 1987.

Mark Girouard, *The Return to Camelot: Chivalry and the English Gentleman*. New Haven and London: Yale University Press, 1981.

J.H. Grainger, *Patriotisms: Britain, 1900–1939*. London: Routledge, 1986.

W.E. Henley, *The Song of the Sword and Other Verses*. London: D. Nutt, 1892.

Maurice Hewlett, *The Letters of Maurice Hewlett; to which is added a Diary in Greece, 1914* edited by Laurence Binyon, with introductory memoir by Edward Hewlett. London: Methuen & Co., 1926.

Amelia Hill, 'Winston Churchill manuscript reveals his poetic side', *The Guardian*, 6 February 2013.

Edmond Holmes, *The Nemesis of Docility: A Study of the German Character*. London: Constable & Co, 1916.

Peter Hopkirk, *The Great Game: On Secret Service in High Asia*. London: John Murray, 1990.

Patrick Howarth, *Play Up and Play the Game: The Heroes of Popular Fiction*. London: Eyre Methuen, 1973.

John Howlett (Ed.), *Invictus: Selected Poems and Prose of W.E. Henley*. Brighton: Sussex Academic Press, 2017.

Lawrence James, *The Savage Wars: British Campaigns in Africa, 1870–1920*. London: Hale, 1985.

Coulson Kernahan, *Six Famous Living Poets: Introductory Studies Illustrated by Quotation and Comment*. London: Thornton Butterworth, 1922.

Rudyard Kipling, *The Five Nations*. London: Methuen, 1903.

Philip Knightley, 'Are We Just a Nation of Born Losers? After England Get Another Drubbing in the Ashes …', *The Daily Mail*, 19 December 2006.

Percy Lubbock, 'Three Poets of To-Day', *The Times Literary Supplement*, 18 November 1909, 436–437.

Andrew Lycett, *Rudyard Kipling*. London: Weidenfeld & Nicholson, 2015.

Frederic William Maitland, *The Life and Letters of Leslie Stephen*. London: Duckworth, 1906.

Michael McGarvie, *The Mystery of Fidele: An Investigation of the Origins and Background of Sir Henry Newbolt's Ballad of Orchardleigh 'Fidele's Grassy Tomb'*. Frome: Frome Society for Local Study, 1999.

Kenneth Millard, *Edwardian Poetry*. Oxford: Clarendon Press, 1991.

Jan Morris, *Farewell the Trumpets: An Imperial Retreat*. London: Faber, 1978.

Paul O'Prey (Ed.), *Poems of Two Wars: Laurence Binyon*. London: Dare-Gale Press, 2016.

INTRODUCTION

Wilfred Owen, *Collected Letters*, edited by Harold Owen and John Bell. London: Oxford University Press, 1967.

Herbert Palmer, *Post Victorian Poetry*. London: Dent, 1938.

John Perry, 'The Teaching of English in England Through the Ages: How Has the Newbolt Report Been Interpreted at Different Times?', *English in Education*, Vol. 53, No. 3 (2019), 240–252.

John Press, *A Map of Modern English Verse*. Oxford: Oxford University Press, 1971.

Paul Readman, 'The Conservative Party, Patriotism, and British Politics: The Case of the General Election of 1900', *Journal of British Studies*, Vol. 40, No.1 (Jan. 2001), 107–145.

H.J. Rose, 'Mr. Henry Newbolt's Verse and Our South African Troops. To the Editor of the "Spectator"', *The Spectator*, 18 October 1902, 565–566.

George Sampson, 'The Reader: Henry Newbolt', *The Bookman*, November 1914, 35–39.

Roger Scruton, *England: An Elegy*. London, New York: Continuum, 2006.

Bernard Semmel, *Imperialism and Social Reform: English Social-Imperial Thought 1895–1914*. London: George Allen & Unwin, 1960.

Malvern Van Wyk Smith, *Drummer Hodge: The Poetry of the Anglo-Boer War (1899–1902)*. Oxford: Clarendon Press, 1978.

Julia Stapleton, 'James Fitzjames Stephen: Liberalism, Patriotism, and English Liberty', *Victorian Studies*, Vol. 41, No. 2 (Winter 1998), 243–263.

Matthew Sweeney (Ed.), *Walter de la Mare: Selected Poems*. London: Faber and Faber, 2006.

David Turner, *The Old Boys: The Decline and Rise of the Public School*. New Haven: Yale University Press, 2015.

Elizabeth Vandiver, *Stand in the Trench, Achilles: Classical Receptions in British Poetry of the Great War*. Oxford: Oxford University Press, 2013.

Theresa Whistler, *Imagination of the Heart: The Life of Walter de la Mare*. London: Duckworth, 1993.

William Wootten, *Reading Walter de la Mare*. London: Faber and Faber, 2021.

Emma Jane Worboise, *The Life of Thomas Arnold D.D.* London: Hamilton, Adams & Co., 1859.

The Poems

from **Admirals All and Other Verses, 1897**

Admirals All

A Song of Sea Kings

EFFINGHAM, Grenville, Raleigh, Drake,
   Here's to the bold and free!
Benbow, Collingwood, Byron, Blake,
   Hail to the Kings of the Sea!
Admirals all, for England's sake,
   Honour be yours and fame!
And honour, as long as waves shall break,
   To Nelson's peerless name!

   Admirals all, for England's sake,
     Honour be yours and fame!
   And honour, as long as waves shall break,
     To Nelson's peerless name!

Essex was fretting in Cadiz Bay
   With the galleons fair in sight;
Howard at last must give him his way,
   And the word was passed to fight.
Never was schoolboy gayer than he,
   Since holidays first began:
He tossed his bonnet to wind and sea,
   And under the guns he ran.

PLAYING THE GAME

Drake nor devil nor Spaniard feared,
   Their cities he put to the sack;
He singed his Catholic Majesty's beard,
   And harried his ships to wrack.
He was playing at Plymouth a rubber of bowls
   When the great Armada came;
But he said, "They must wait their turn, good souls,"
   And he stooped, and finished the game.

Fifteen sail were the Dutchmen bold,
   Duncan he had but two:
But he anchored them fast where the Texel shoaled
   And his colours aloft he flew.
"I've taken the depth to a fathom," he cried,
   "And I'll sink with a right good will,
For I know when we're all of us under the tide,
   My flag will be fluttering still."

Splinters were flying above, below,
   When Nelson sailed the Sound:
"Mark you, I wouldn't be elsewhere now,"
   Said he, "for a thousand pound!"
The Admiral's signal bade him fly,
   But he wickedly wagged his head,
He clapped the glass to his sightless eye
   And "I'm damned if I see it," he said.

Admirals all, they said their say
   (The echoes are ringing still),
Admirals all, they went their way
   To the haven under the hill.
But they left us a kingdom none can take,
   The realm of the circling sea,
To be ruled by the rightful sons of Blake
   And the Rodneys yet to be.

Admirals all, for England's sake,
   Honour be yours and fame!
And honour, as long as waves shall break,
   To Nelson's peerless name!

THE POEMS

San Stefano

(A ballad of the bold *Menelaus*)

IT was morning at St. Helen's, in the great and gallant
    days,
  And the sea beneath the sun glittered wide,
When the frigate set her courses, all a-shimmer in the
    haze,
  And she hauled her cable home and took the tide.
She'd a right fighting company, three hundred men and
    more,
  Nine and forty guns in tackle running free;
And they cheered her from the shore for her colours at
    the fore,
  When the bold *Menelaus* put to sea.

She'd a right fighting company, three hundred men and more,
  Nine and forty guns in tackle running free;
And they cheered her from the shore for her colours at the fore,
  When the bold Menelaus *put to sea.*

She was clear of Monte Cristo, she was heading for the
    land,
  When she spied a pennant red and white and blue;
They were foeman, and they knew it, and they'd half a
    league in hand,
  But she flung aloft her royals and she flew.
She was nearer, nearer, nearer, they were caught beyond
    a doubt,
  But she slipped her, into Orbetello Bay,
And the lubbers gave a shout as they paid their cables
    out,
  With the guns grinning round them where they lay.

Now Sir Peter was a captain of a famous fighting race,
  Son and grandson of an admiral was he;
And he looked upon the batteries, he looked upon the
    chase,
  And he heard the shout that echoed out to sea.
And he called across the decks, "Ay! the cheering might
    be late
  If they kept it till the *Menelaus* runs;

Bid the master and his mate heave the lead and lay her
      straight
For the prize lying yonder by the guns."

When the summer moon was setting, into Ortobello
      Bay
  Came the *Menelaus* gliding like a ghost;
And her boats were manned in silence, and in silence
      pulled away,
  And in silence every gunner took his post.
With a volley from her broadside the citadel she woke,
  And they hammered back like heroes all the night;
But before the morning broke she had vanished through
      the smoke
  With her prize upon her quarter grappled tight.

It was evening at St. Helen's, in the great and gallant
      time,
  And the sky behind the down was flushing far;
And the flags were all a-flutter, and the bells were all
      a-chime,
  When the frigate cast her anchor off the bar.
She'd a right fighting company, three hundred men and
      more,
  Nine and forty guns in tackle running free;
And they cheered her from the shore for her colours at
      the fore,
  When the bold *Menelaus* came from sea.

She'd a right fighting company, three hundred men and more,
  Nine and forty guns in tackle running free;
And they cheered her from the shore for her colours at the fore,
  When the bold Menelaus *came from sea.*

Drake's Drum

DRAKE he's in his hammock an' a thousand mile away,
  (Capten, art tha sleepin' there below?),
Slung atween the round shot in Nombre Dios Bay,
  An' dreamin' arl the time o' Plymouth Hoe.
Yarnder lumes the Island, yarnder lie the ships,
  Wi' sailor lads a-dancin' heel-an'-toe,

An' the shore-lights flashin', an' the night-tide dashin',
   He sees et arl so plainly as he saw et long ago.

Drake he was a Devon man, an' rüled the Devon seas,
   (Capten, art tha' sleepin' there below?),
Rovin' tho' his death fell, he went wi' heart at ease,
   An' dreamin' arl the time o' Plymouth Hoe.
"Take my drum to England, hang et by the shore,
   Strike et when your powder's runnin' low;
If the Dons sight Devon, I'll quit the port o' Heaven,
   An' drum them up the Channel as we drummed them long ago."

Drake he's in his hammock till the great Armadas come,
   (Capten, art tha' sleepin' there below?),
Slung atween the round shot, listenin' for the drum,
   An' dreamin arl the time o' Plymouth Hoe.
Call him on the deep sea, call him up the Sound,
   Call him when ye sail to meet the foe;
Where the old trade's plyin' an' the old flag flyin'
   They shall find him ware an' wakin', as they found him long ago!

Hawke

IN seventeen hundred and fifty nine,
   When Hawke came swooping from the West,
The French King's Admiral with twenty of the line,
   Was sailing forth, to sack us, out of Brest.
The ports of France were crowded, the quays of France a-hum
With thirty thousand soldiers marching to the drum,
For bragging time was over and fighting time was come
   When Hawke came swooping from the West.

'Twas long past noon of a wild November day
   When Hawke came swooping from the West;
He heard the breakers thundering in Quiberon Bay,
   But he flew the flag for battle, line abreast.
Down upon the quicksands roaring out of sight
Fiercely beat the storm-wind, darkly fell the night,
But they took the foe for pilot and the cannon's glare for light
   When Hawke came swooping from the West.

The Frenchmen turned like a covey down the wind
  When Hawke came swooping from the West;
One he sank with all hands, one he caught and pinned,
  And the shallows and the storm took the rest.
The guns that should have conquered us they rusted on
    the shore,
The men that would have mastered us they drummed and
    marched no more,
For England was England, and a mighty brood she bore
  When Hawke came swooping from the West.

The Fighting Téméraire

IT was eight bells ringing,
  For the morning watch was done,
And the gunner's lads were singing
  As they polished every gun.
It was eight bells ringing,
And the gunner's lads were singing,
For the ship she rode a-swinging
  As they polished every gun.

   Oh! to see the linstock lighting,
    Téméraire! Téméraire!
   Oh! to hear the round shot biting,
    Téméraire! Téméraire!
   Oh! to see the linstock lighting,
   And to hear the round shot biting,
   For we're all in love with fighting
    On the fighting Téméraire.

It was noontide ringing,
  And the battle just begun,
When the ship her way was winging
  As they loaded every gun.
It was noontide ringing,
When the ship her way was winging,
And the gunner's lads were singing
  As they loaded every gun.

   There'll be many grim and gory,
    Téméraire! Téméraire!

There'll be few to tell the story,
  Téméraire! Téméraire!

There'll be many grim and gory,
There'll be few to tell the story,
But we'll all be one in glory
  With the Fighting Téméraire.

There's a far bell ringing
  At the setting of the sun,
And a phantom voice is singing
  Of the great days done.
There's a far bell ringing,
And a phantom voice is singing
Of renown for ever clinging
  To the great days done.

Now the sunset breezes shiver,
  Téméraire! Téméraire!
And she's fading down the river,
  Téméraire! Téméraire!
Now the sunset's breezes shiver,
And she's fading down the river,
But in England's song for ever
  She's the Fighting Téméraire.

Vitaï Lampada

THERE'S a breathless hush in the Close to-night—
  Ten to make and the match to win—
A bumping pitch and a blinding light,
  An hour to play and the last man in.
And it's not for the sake of a ribboned coat,
  Or the selfish hope of a season's fame,
But his Captain's hand on his shoulder smote—
  "Play up! play up! and play the game!"

The sand of the desert is sodden red,—
  Red with the wreck of a square that broke; —
The Gatling's jammed and the Colonel dead,
  And the regiment blind with dust and smoke.
The river of death has brimmed his banks,
  And England's far, and Honour a name,

But the voice of a schoolboy rallies the ranks:
  "Play up! play up! and play the game!"

This is the word that year by year,
  While in her place the School is set,
Every one of her sons must hear,
  And none that hears it dare forget.
This they all with a joyful mind
  Bear through life like a torch in flame,
And falling fling to the host behind—
  "Play up! play up! and play the game!"

He Fell Among Thieves

"YE have robbed," said he, "ye have slaughtered and made an end,
  Take your ill-got plunder, and bury the dead:
What will ye more of your guest and sometime friend?"
  "Blood for our blood," they said.

He laughed: "If one may settle the score for five,
  I am ready; but let the reckoning stand till day:
I have loved the sunlight as dearly as any alive."
  "You shall die at dawn," said they.

He flung his empty revolver down the slope,
  He climbed alone to the Eastward edge of the trees;
All night long in a dream untroubled of hope
  He brooded, clasping his knees.

He did not hear the monotonous roar that fills
  The ravine where the Yassin river sullenly flows;
He did not see the starlight on the Laspur hills,
  Or the far Afghan snows.

He saw the April noon on his books aglow,
  The wistaria trailing in at the window wide;
He heard his father's voice from the terrace below
  Calling him down to ride.

He saw the gray little church across the park,
  The mounds that hide the loved and honoured dead;
The Norman arch, the chancel softly dark,
  The brasses black and red.

He saw the School Close, sunny and green,
  The runner beside him, the stand by the parapet wall,

The distant tape, and the crowd roaring between
    His own name over all.

He saw the dark wainscot and timbered roof,
    The long tables, and the faces merry and keen;
The College Eight and their trainer dining aloof,
    The Dons on the daïs serene.

He watched the liner's stem ploughing the foam,
    He felt her trembling speed and the thrash of her screw;
He heard her passengers' voices talking of home,
    He saw the flag she flew.

And now it was dawn. He rose strong on his feet,
    And strode to his ruined camp below the wood;
He drank the breath of the morning cool and sweet;
    His murderers round him stood.

Light on the Laspur hills was broadening fast,
    The blood-red snow-peaks chilled to a dazzling white:
He turned, and saw the golden circle at last,
    Cut by the Eastern height.

"O glorious Life, Who dwellest in earth and sun,
    I have lived, I praise and adore Thee."
                                A sword swept.
Over the pass the voices one by one
    Faded, and the hill slept.

Ionicus

I live—I am old— I return to the ground—
Blow trumpets! and still I can dream to the sound.
                                WILLIAM CORY.

WITH failing feet and shoulders bowed
    Beneath the weight of happier days,
He lagged among the heedless crowd,
    Or crept along suburban ways.
But still through all his heart was young,
    His mood a joy that nought could mar,

A courage, a pride, a rapture, sprung
    Of the strength and splendour of England's war.

From ill-requited toil he turned
    To ride with Picton and with Pack,
Among his grammars inly burned
    To storm the Afghan mountain-track.
When midnight chimed, before Quebec
    He watched with Wolfe till the morning star;
At noon he saw from *Victory*'s deck
    The sweep and splendour of England's war.

Beyond the book his teaching sped,
    He left on whom he taught the trace
Of kinship with the deathless dead,
    And faith in all the Island Race.
He passed: his life a tangle seemed,
    His age from fame and power was far;
But his heart was high to the end, and dreamed
    Of the sound and splendour of England's war.

Minora Sidera

(The Dictionary of National Biography)

SITTING at times over a hearth that burns
    With dull domestic glow,
My thought, leaving the book, gratefully turns
    To you who planned it so.

Not of the great only you deigned to tell—
    The stars by which we steer—
But lights out of the night that flashed, and fell
    To night again, are here.

Such as were those, dogs of an elder day,
    Who sacked the golden ports,
And those later who dared grapple their prey
    Beneath the harbour forts:

Some with flag at the fore, sweeping the world
    To find an equal fight,

And some who joined war to their trade, and hurled
    Ships of the line in flight.

Whether their fame centuries long should ring
    They cared not over-much,
But cared greatly to serve God and the king,
    And keep the Nelson touch;

And fought to build Britain above the tide
    Of wars and windy fate;
And passed content, leaving to us the pride
    Of lives obscurely great.

from The Island Race, 1898

The Vigil

ENGLAND! where the sacred flame
   Burns before the inmost shrine,
Where the lips that love thy name
   Consecrate their hopes and thine,
Where the banners of thy dead
Weave their shadows overhead,
Watch beside thine arms to-night,
Pray that God defend the Right.

Think that when to-morrow comes
   War shall claim command of all,
Thou must hear the roll of drums,
   Thou must hear the trumpet's call.
Now before they silence ruth,
Commune with the voice of truth;
England! on thy knees to-night
Pray that God defend the Right.

Hast thou counted up the cost,
   What to foeman, what to friend?
Glory sought is Honour lost,
   How should this be knighthood's end?
Know'st thou what is Hatred's meed?
What the surest gain of Greed?
England! wilt thou dare to-night
Pray that God defend the Right?

Single-hearted, unafraid,
   Hither all thy heroes came,
On this altar's steps were laid
   Gordon's life and Outram's fame.
England! if thy will be yet
By their great example set,
Here beside thine arms to-night
Pray that God defend the Right.

So shalt thou when morning comes
   Rise to conquer or to fall,
Joyful hear the rolling drums,

    Joyful hear the trumpets call.
Then let Memory tell thy heart;
"England! what thou wert, thou art!"
Gird thee with thine ancient might,
Forth! and God defend the Right!

Admiral Death

BOYS, are ye calling a toast to-night?
   (Hear what the sea-wind saith)
Fill for a bumper strong and bright,
   And here's to Admiral Death!
He's sailed in a hundred builds o' boat,
He's fought in a thousand kinds o' coat,
He's the senior flag of all that float,
   And his name's Admiral Death!

Which of you looks for a service free?
   (Hear what the sea-wind saith)
The rules o' the service are but three
   When ye sail with Admiral Death.
Steady your hand in time o' squalls,
Stand to the last by him that falls,
And answer clear to the voice that calls,
   "Ay, ay! Admiral Death!"

How will ye know him among the rest?
   (Hear what the sea-wind saith)
By the glint o' the stars that cover his breast
   Ye may find Admiral Death.
By the forehead grim with an ancient scar,
By the voice that rolls like thunder far,
By the tenderest eyes of all that are,
   Ye may know Admiral Death.

Where are the lads that sailed before?
   (Hear what the sea-wind saith)
Their bones are white by many a shore,
   They sleep with Admiral Death.
Oh! but they loved him, young and old,
For he left the laggard, and took the bold,
And the fight was fought, and the story's told,
   And they sleep with Admiral Death.

Messmates

HE gave us all a good-bye cheerily
  At the first dawn of day;
We dropped him down the side full drearily
  When the light died away.
It's a dead dark watch that he's a-keeping there,
And a long, long night that lags a-creeping there,
Where the Trades and the tides roll over him
  And the great ships go by.

He's there alone with green seas rocking him
  For a thousand miles round;
He's there alone with dumb things mocking him,
  And we're homeward bound.
It's a long, lone watch that he's a-keeping there,
And a dead cold night that lags a-creeping there,
While the months and the years roll over him
  And the great ships go by.

I wonder if the tramps come near enough
  As they thrash to and fro,
And the battle-ships' bells ring clear enough
  To be heard down below;
If through all the lone watch that he's a-keeping there,
And the long, cold night that lags a-creeping there,
The voices of the sailor-men shall comfort him
  When the great ships go by.

The Death of Admiral Blake

(August 7th, 1657)

LADEN with spoil of the South, fulfilled with the
    glory of achievement,
  And freshly crowned with never-dying fame,
Sweeping by shores where the names of
    the victories of England,
  Across the Bay the squadron homeward came.

Proudly they came, but their pride was the pomp of a
    funeral at midnight,

When dreader yet the lonely morrow looms;
Few are the words that are spoken, and faces are gaunt
    beneath the torchlight
  That does but darken more the nodding plumes.

Low on the field of his fame, past hope lay the Admiral
    triumphant,
  And fain to rest him after all his pain;
Yet for the love that he bore to his own land, ever
    unforgotten,
  He prayed to see the western hills again.

Fainter than stars in a sky long gray with the coming of
    the daybreak,
  Or sounds of night that fade when night is done,
So in the death-dawn faded the splendour and loud
    renown of warfare,
  And life of all its longings kept but one.

"Oh! to be there for an hour when the shade draws in
    beside the hedgerows,
  And falling apples wake the drowsy noon:
Oh! for the hour when the elms grow sombre and
    human in the twilight,
  And gardens dream beneath the rising moon.

"Only to look once more on the land of the memories
    of childhood,
  Forgetting weary winds and barren foam:
Only to bid farewell to the combe and the orchard and
    the moorland,
  And sleep at last among the fields of home!"

So he was silently praying, till now, when his strength
    was ebbing faster,
  The Lizard lay before them faintly blue;
Now on the gleaming horizon the white cliffs laughed
    along the coast-line,
  And now the forelands took the shapes they knew.

There lay the Sound and the Island with green leaves
    down beside the water,
  The town, the Hoe, the masts with sunset fired—
Dreams! ay, dreams of the dead! for the great heart
    faltered on the threshold,
  And darkness took the land his soul desired.

The Non-Combatant

AMONG a race high-handed, strong of heart,
Sea-rovers, conquerors, builders in the waste,
He had his birth; a nature too complete,
Eager and doubtful, no man's soldier sworn
And no man's chosen captain; born to fail,
A name without an echo: yet he too
Within the cloister of his narrow days
Fulfilled the ancestral rites, and kept alive
The eternal fire; it may be, not in vain;
For out of those who dropped a downward glance
Upon the weakling huddled at his prayers,
Perchance some looked beyond him, and then first
Beheld the glory, and what shrine it filled,
And to what Spirit sacred: or perchance
Some heard him chanting, though but to himself,
The old heroic names: and went their way:
And hummed his music on the march to death.

Clifton Chapel

THIS is the Chapel: here, my son,
   Your father thought the thoughts of youth,
And heard the words that one by one
   The touch of Life has turned to truth.
Here, in a day that is not far,
   You too may speak with noble ghosts
Of manhood and the vows of war
   You made before the Lord of Hosts.

To set the cause above renown,
   To love the game beyond the prize,
To honour, while you strike him down,
   The foe that comes with fearless eyes;
To count the life of battle good,
   And dear the land that gave you birth,
And dearer yet the brotherhood
   That binds the brave of all the earth—

My son, the oath is yours: the end
   Is His, Who built the world of strife,
Who gave His children Pain for friend,
   And Death for surest hope of life.
To-day and here the fight's begun,
   Of the great fellowship you're free;
Henceforth the School and you are one,
   And what You are, the race shall be.

God send you fortune: yet be sure,
   Among the lights that gleam and pass,
You'll live to follow none more pure
   Than that which glows on yonder brass.
"Qui procul hinc" the legend's writ,—
   The frontier-grave is far away—
    "Qui ante diem periit:
    Sed miles, sed pro patriâ."

The Echo

OF A BALLAD SUNG BY H. PLUNKET GREENE TO HIS OLD SCHOOL

TWICE three hundred boys were we,
   Long ago, long ago,
Where the Downs look out to the Severn Sea.
   Clifton for aye!
We held by the game and hailed the team,
For many could play where few could dream.
   City of Song shall stand alway.

Some were for profit and some for pride,
   Long ago, long ago,
Some for the flag they lived and died.
   Clifton for aye!
The work of the world must still be done,
And minds are many though truth be one.
   City of Song shall stand alway.

But a lad there was to his fellows sang,
   Long ago, long ago,
And soon the world to his music rang.
   Clifton for aye!

PLAYING THE GAME

Follow your Captains, crown your Kings,
But what will ye give to the lad that sings?
  City of Song shall stand alway.

For the voice ye hear is the voice of home,
  Long ago, long ago,
And the voice of Youth with the world to roam.
  Clifton for aye!
The voice of passion and human tears,
And the voice of the vision that lights the years.
  City of Song shall stand alway.

Fidele's Grassy Tomb

THE squire sat propped in a pillowed chair,
His eyes were alive and clear of care,
But well he knew that the hour was come
To bid good-bye to his ancient home.

He looked on garden, wood, and hill,
He looked on the lake, sunny and still:
The last of earth that his eyes could see
Was the island church of Orchardleigh.

The last that his heart could understand
Was the touch of the tongue that licked his hand:
"Bury the dog at my feet," he said,
And his voice dropped, and the Squire was dead.

Now the dog was a hound of the Danish breed,
Staunch to love and strong at need:
He had dragged his master safe to shore
When the tide was ebbing at Elsinore.

From that day forth, as reason would,
He was named "Fidele," and made it good:
When the last of the mourners left the door
Fidele was dead on the chantry floor.

They buried him there at his master's feet,
And all that heard of it deemed it meet:
The story went the round for years,
Till it came at last to the Bishop's ears.

Bishop of Bath and Wells was he,
Lord of the lords of Orchardleigh;
And he wrote to the Parson the strongest screed
That Bishop may write or Parson read.

The sum of it was that a soulless hound
Was known to be buried in hallowed ground:
From scandal sore the Church to save
They must take the dog from his master's grave.

The heir was far in a foreign land,
The Parson was wax to my Lord's command:
He sent for the Sexton and bade him make
A lonely grave by the shore of the lake.

The Sexton sat by the water's brink
Where he used to sit when he used to think:
He reasoned slow, but he reasoned it out,
And his argument left him free from doubt.

"A Bishop," he said, "is the top of his trade;
But there's others can give him a start with the spade:
Yon dog, he carried the Squire ashore,
And a Christian couldn't ha' done no more."

The grave was dug; the mason came
And carved on stone Fidele's name;
But the dog that the Sexton laid inside
Was a dog that never had lived or died.

So the Parson was praised, and the scandal stayed,
Till, a long time after, the church decayed,
And, laying the floor anew, they found
In the tomb of the Squire the bones of a hound.

As for the Bishop of Bath and Wells
No more of him the story tells;
Doubtless he lived as a Prelate and Prince,
And died and was buried a century since.

And whether his view was right or wrong
Has little to do with this my song;
Something we owe him, you must allow;
And perhaps he has changed his mind by now.

The Squire in the family chantry sleeps,
The marble still his memory keeps:

Remember, when the name you spell,
There rest Fidele's bones as well.

For the Sexton's grave you need not search,
'Tis a nameless mound by the island church:
An ignorant fellow, of humble lot—
But he knew one thing that a Bishop did not.

Imogen

(A Lady of Tender Age)

LADIES, where were your bright eyes glancing,
   Where were they glancing yesternight?
Saw ye Imogen dancing, dancing,
   Imogen dancing all in white?
   Laughed she not with a pure delight,
   Laughed she not with a joy serene,
Stepped she not with a grace entrancing,
   Slenderly girt in silken sheen?

All thorough the night from dusk to daytime
   Under her feet the hours were swift,
Under her feet the hours of playtime
   Rose and fell with a rhythmic lift:
   Music set her adrift, adrift,
   Music eddying towards the day
Swept her along as brooks in Maytime
   Carry the freshly falling May.

Ladies, life is a changing measure,
   Youth is a lilt that endeth soon;
Pluck ye never so fast at pleasure,
   Twilight follows the longest noon.
   Nay, but here is a lasting boon,
   Life for hearts that are old and chill,
Youth undying for hearts that treasure
   Imogen dancing, dancing still.

Nel Mozzo del Cammín

WHISPER it not that late in years
Sorrow shall fade and the world be brighter,
Life be freed of tremor and tears,
Heads be wiser and hearts be lighter.
Ah! but the dream that all endears,
The dream we sell for your pottage of truth—
Give us again the passion of youth,
Sorrow shall fade and the world be brighter.

The Invasion

SPRING, they say, with his greenery
    Northward marches at last,
        Mustering thorn and elm;
Breezes rumour him conquering,
    Tell how Victory sits
        High on his glancing helm.

Smit with sting of his archery,
    Hardest ashes and oaks
        Burn at the root below:
Primrose, violet, daffodil,
    Start like blood where the shafts
        Light from his golden bow.

Here where winter oppresses us
    Still we listen and doubt,
        Dreading a hope betrayed:
Sore we long to be greeting him,
    Still we linger and doubt
        "What if his march be stayed?"

Folk in thrall to the enemy,
    Vanquished, tilling a soil
        Hateful and hostile grown;
Always wearily, warily,
    Feeding deep in the heart
        Passion they dare not own—

So we wait the deliverer;
        Surely soon shall he come,
            Soon shall his hour be due:
Spring shall come with his greenery,
        Life be lovely again,
            Earth be the home we knew.

Ireland, Ireland

DOWN thy valleys, Ireland, Ireland,
   Down thy valleys green and sad,
Still thy spirit wanders wailing,
   Wanders wailing, wanders mad.

Long ago that anguish took thee,
   Ireland, Ireland, green and fair,
Spoilers strong in darkness took thee,
   Broke thy heart and left thee there.

Down thy valleys, Ireland, Ireland,
   Still thy spirit wanders mad;
All too late they love that wronged thee,
   Ireland, Ireland, green and sad.

Moonset

PAST seven o'clock: time to be gone;
Twelfth-night's over and dawn shivering up:
A hasty cut of the loaf, a steaming cup,
Down to the door, and there is Coachman John.

Ruddy of cheek is John and bright of eye;
But John it appears has none of your grins and winks;
Civil enough, but short: perhaps he thinks:
Words come once in a mile, and always dry.

Has he a mind or not? I wonder; but soon
We turn through a leafless wood, and there to the right,
Like a sun bewitched in alien realms of night,
Mellow and yellow and rounded hangs the moon.

Strangely near she seems, and terribly great:
The world is dead: why are we travelling still?
Nightmare silence grips my struggling will;
We are driving for ever and ever to find a gate.

"When you come to consider the moon," says John at last,
And stops, to feel his footing and take his stand;
"And then there's some will say there's never a hand
That made the world!"
      A flick, and the gates are passed.

Out of the dim magical moonlit park,
Out to the workday road and wider skies:
There's a warm flush in the East where day's to rise,
And I'm feeling the better for Coachman John's remark.

from The Sailing of the Long-Ships and Other Poems, 1902

The Sailing of the Long-Ships

(October, 1899)

THEY saw the cables loosened, they saw the gangways cleared,
They heard the women weeping, they heard the men that cheered;
Far off, far off, the tumult faded and died away,
And all alone the sea-wind came singing up the Bay.

"I came by Cape St. Vincent, I came by Trafalgar,
I swept from Torres Vedras to golden Vigo Bar,
I saw the beacons blazing that fired the world with light
When down their ancient highway your fathers passed to fight.

"O race of tireless fighters, flushed with a youth renewed,
Right well the wars of Freedom befit the Sea-kings' brood;
Yet as ye go forget not the fame of yonder shore,
The fame ye owe your fathers and the old time before.

"Long-suffering were the Sea-kings, they were not swift to kill,
But when the sands had fallen they waited no man's will;
Though all the world forbade them, they counted not nor cared,
They weighed not help or hindrance, they did the thing they dared.

"The Sea-kings loved not boasting, they cursed not him that cursed,
They honoured all men duly, and him that faced them, first;
They strove and knew not hatred, they smote and toiled to save,
They tended whom they vanquished, they praised the fallen brave.

"Their fame's on Torres Vedras, their fame's on Vigo Bar,
Far-flashed to Cape St. Vincent it burns from Trafalgar;
Mark as ye go the beacons that woke the world with light
When down their ancient highway your fathers passed to fight."

Waggon Hill

DRAKE in the North Sea grimly prowling,
    Treading his dear *Revenge*'s deck,
Watched, with the sea-dogs round him growling,
    Galleons drifting wreck by wreck.
    "Fetter and Faith for England's neck,
   Faggot and Father, Saint and chain,—
Yonder the Devil and all go howling,
    Devon, O Devon, in wind and rain!"

Drake at the last off Nombre lying,
    Knowing the night that toward him crept,
Gave to the sea-dogs round him crying
    This for a sign before he slept:—
    "Pride of the West! What Devon hath kept
   Devon shall keep on tide or main;
Call to the storm and drive them flying,
    Devon, O Devon, in wind and rain!"

Valour of England gaunt and whitening,
    Far in a South land brought to bay,
Locked in a death-grip all day tightening,
    Waited the end in twilight gray.
    Battle and storm and the sea-dog's way!
   Drake from his long rest turned again,
Victory lit thy steel with lightning,
    Devon, O Devon, in wind and rain!

The Volunteer

"HE leapt to arms unbidden,
    Unneeded, over-bold;
His face by earth is hidden,
    His heart in earth is cold.

"Curse on the reckless daring
    That could not wait the call,
The proud fantastic bearing
    That would be first to fall!"

O tears of human passion,
   Blur not the image true;
This was not folly's fashion,
   This was the man we knew.

The Schoolfellow

OUR game was his but yesteryear;
   We wished him back; we could not know
The selfsame hour we missed him here
   He led the line that broke the foe.

Blood-red behind our guarded posts
   Sank as of old the dying day;
The battle ceased; the mingled hosts
   Weary and cheery went their way:

"To-morrow well may bring," we said,
   "As fair a fight, as clear a sun."
Dear lad, before the word was sped,
For evermore thy goal was won.

The Only Son

O BITTER wind toward the sunset blowing
   What of the dales to-night?
In yonder gray old hall what fires are glowing,
   What ring of festal light?

"In the great window as the day was dwindling
   I saw an old man stand;
His head was proudly held and his eyes kindling,
   But the list shook in his hand."

O wind of twilight, was there no word uttered,
   No sound of joy or wail?
"'A great fight and a good death,' he muttered;
   'Trust him, he would not fail.'"

What of the chamber dark where she was lying
    For whom all life is done?
"Within her heart she rocks a dead child, crying
    'My son, my little son.'"

The School at War

ALL night before the brink of death
    In fitful sleep the army lay,
For through the dream that stilled their breath
    Too gauntly glared the coming day.

But we, within whose blood there leaps
    The fullness of a life as wide
As Avon's water where he sweeps
    Seaward at last with Severn's tide,

We heard beyond the desert night
    The murmur of the fields we knew,
And our swift souls with one delight
    Like homing swallows Northward flew.

We played again the immortal games,
    And grappled with the fierce old friends,
And cheered the dead undying names,
    And sang the song that never ends;

Till, when the hard, familiar bell
    Told that the summer night was late,
Where long ago we said farewell
    We said farewell by the old gate.

"O Captains unforgot," they cried,
    "Come you again or come no more,
Across the world you keep the pride,
    Across the world we mark the score."

By the Hearth-Stone

BY the hearth-stone
She sits alone,
   The long night bearing:
With eyes that gleam
Into the dream
   Of the firelight staring.

Low and more low
The dying glow
   Burns in the embers;
She nothing heeds
And nothing needs—
   Only remembers.

Commemoration

I SAT by the granite pillar, and sunlight fell
   Where the sunlight fell of old,
And the hour was the hour my heart remembered well,
   And the sermon rolled and rolled
As it used to roll when the place was still unhaunted,
   And the strangest tale in the world was still untold.

And I knew that of all this rushing of urgent sound
   That I so clearly heard,
The green young forest of saplings clustered round
   Was heeding not one word:
Their heads were bowed in a still serried patience
   Such as an angel's breath could never have stirred.

For some were already away to the hazardous pitch,
   Or lining the parapet wall,
And some were in glorious battle, or great and rich,
   Or throned in a college hall:
And among the rest was one like my own young phantom,
   Dreaming for ever beyond my utmost call.

"O Youth," the preacher was crying, "deem not thou
   Thy life is thine alone;
Thou bearest the will of the ages, seeing how
   They built thee bone by bone,

And within thy blood the Great Age sleeps sepulchred
    Till thou and thine shall roll away the stone.

"Therefore the days are coming when thou shalt burn
     With passion whitely hot;
Rest shall be rest no more; thy feet shall spurn
     All that thy hand hath got;
And One that is stronger shall gird thee, and lead thee swiftly
      Whither, O heart of Youth, thou wouldest not."

And the School passed: and I saw the living and dead
     Set in their seats again,
And I longed to hear them speak of the word that was said,
     But I knew that I longed in vain.
And they stretched forth their hands, and the wind of the spirit took them
     Lightly as drifted leaves on an endless plain.

The Nile

OUT of the unknown South,
Through the dark lands of drouth,
   Far wanders ancient Nile in slumber gliding:
Clear-mirrored in his dream
The deeds that haunt his stream
   Flash out and fade like stars in midnight sliding.
Long since, before the life of man
   Rose from among the lives that creep,
With Time's own tide began
   That still mysterious sleep,
   Only to cease when Time shall reach the eternal deep.

From out his vision vast
The early gods have passed,
   They waned and perished with the faith that made them;
The long phantasmal line
Of Pharaohs crowned divine
   Are dust among the dust that once obeyed them.
Their land is one mute burial mound,
   Save when across the drifted years
Some chant of hollow sound,
   Some triumph blent with tears,
   From Memnon's lips at dawn wakens the desert meres.

O Nile, and can it be
No memory dwells with thee
   Of Grecian lore and the sweet Grecian singer?
The legions' iron tramp,
The Goths' wide-wandering camp,
   Had these no fame that by thy shore might linger?
Nay, then must all be lost indeed,
   Lost too the swift pursuing might
That cleft with passionate speed
   Aboukir's tranquil night,
   And shattered in mid-swoop the great world-eagle's flight.

Yet have there been on earth
Spirits of starry birth,
   Whose splendour rushed to no eternal setting:
They over all endure,
Their course through all is sure,
   The dark world's light is still of their begetting.
Though the long past forgotten lies,
   Nile! in thy dream remember him,
Whose like no more shall rise
   Above our twilight's rim,
   Until the immortal dawn shall make all glories dim.

For this man was not great
By gold or kingly state,
   Or the bright sword, or knowledge of earth's wonder;
But more than all his race
He saw life face to face,
   And heard the still small voice above the thunder.
O river, while thy waters roll
   By yonder vast deserted tomb,
There, where so clear a soul
   So shone through gathering doom,
Thou and thy land shall keep the tale of lost Khartoum.

Outward Bound

DEAR Earth, near Earth, the clay that made us men,
   The land we sowed,
     The hearth that glowed—
       O Mother, must we bid farewell to thee?

Fast dawns the last dawn, and what shall comfort then
    The lonely hearts that roam the outer sea?

Gray wakes the daybreak, the shivering sails are set,
  To misty deeps
  The channel sweeps—
    O Mother, think on us who think on thee!
Earth-home, birth-home, with love remember yet
    The sons in exile on the eternal sea.

From Generation to Generation

O SON of mine, when dusk shall find thee bending
    Between a gravestone and a cradle's head—
Between the love whose name is loss unending
    And the young love whose thoughts are liker dread,—
Thou too shalt groan at heart that all thy spending
    Cannot repay the dead, the hungry dead.

When I Remember

WHEN I remember that the day will come
    For this our love to quit his land of birth,
    And bid farewell to all the ways of earth
With lips that must for evermore be dumb,

Then creep I silent from the stirring hum,
    And shut away the music and the mirth,
    And reckon up what may be left of worth
When hearts are cold and love's own body numb.

Something there must be that I know not here,
Or know too dimly through the symbol dear;
    Some touch, some beauty, only guessed by this—
If He that made us loves, it shall replace,
Beloved, even the vision of thy face
    And deep communion of thine inmost kiss.

The Viking's Song

WHEN I thy lover first
   Shook out my canvas free
And like a pirate burst
   Into that dreaming sea,
The land knew no such thirst
   As then tormented me.

Now when at eve returned
   I near that shore divine,
Where once but watch-fires burned
   I see thy beacon shine,
And know the land hath learned
   Desire that welcomes mine.

Yattendon

AMONG the woods and tillage
   That fringe the topmost downs,
All lonely lies the village,
   Far off from seas and towns.
Yet when her own folk slumbered
   I heard within her street
Murmur of men unnumbered
   And march of myriad feet.

For all she lies so lonely,
   Far off from towns and seas,
The village holds not only
   The roofs beneath her trees:
While Life is sweet and tragic
   And Death is veiled and dumb,
Hither, by singer's magic,
   The pilgrim world must come.

A Sower

WITH sanguine looks
   And rolling walk
Among the rooks
   He loved to stalk,

While on the land
   With gusty laugh
From a full hand
   He scattered chaff.

Now that within
   His spirit sleeps
A harvest thin
   The sickle reaps;

But the dumb fields
   Desire his tread,
And no earth yields
   A wheat more red.

Northumberland

"The Old and Bold"

WHEN England sets her banner forth
   And bids her armour shine,
She'll not forget the famous North,
   The lads of moor and Tyne;
And when the loving-cup's in hand,
   And Honour leads the cry,
They know not old Northumberland
   Who'll pass her memory by.

When Nelson sailed for Trafalgar
   With all his country's best,
He held them dear as brothers are,
   But one beyond the rest.
For when the fleet with heroes manned
   To clear the decks began,

The boast of old Northumberland
    He sent to lead the van.

Himself by *Victory*'s bulwarks stood
    And cheered to see the sight;
"That noble fellow Collingwood,
    How bold he goes to fight!"
Love, that the league of Ocean spanned,
    Heard him as face to face;
"What would he give, Northumberland,
    To share our pride of place?"

The flag that goes the world around
    And flaps on every breeze
Has never gladdened fairer ground
    Or kinder hearts than these.
So when the loving-cup's in hand
    And Honour leads the cry,
They know not old Northumberland
    Who'll pass her memory by.

THE POEMS

from Songs of Memory and Hope, 1909

Sacrementum Supremum

YE that with me have fought and failed and fought
    To the last desperate trench of battle's crest,
Not yet to sleep, not yet; our work is nought;
    On that last trench the fate of all may rest.
Draw near, my friends; and let your thoughts be high;
    Great hearts are glad when it is time to give;
Life is no life to him that dares not die,
    And death no death to him that dares to live.

Draw near together; none be last or first;
    We are no longer names, but one desire;
With the same burning of the soul we thirst,
    And the same wine to-night shall quench our fire.
Drink! to our fathers who begot us men,
    To the dead voices that are never dumb;
Then to the land of all our loves, and then
    To the long parting, and the age to come.

Devon

DEEP-WOODED combes, clear-mounded hills of morn,
Red sunset tides against a red sea-wall,
    High lonely barrows where the curlews call,
Far moors that echo to the ringing horn,—
Devon! thou spirit of all these beauties born,
    All these are thine, but thou art more than all:
    Speech can but tell thy name, praise can but fall
Beneath the cold white sea-mist of thy scorn.

Yet, yet, O noble land, forbid us not
    Even now to join our faint memorial chime
To the fierce chant wherewith their hearts were hot
    Who took the tide in thy Imperial prime;
Whose glory's thine till Glory sleeps forgot
    With her ancestral phantoms, Pride and Time.

The Mossrose

WALKING to-day in your garden, O gracious lady,
Little you thought as you turned in that alley remote and shady,
And gave me a rose and asked if I knew its savour—
The old-world scent of the mossrose, flower of a bygone favour—

Little you thought as you waited the word of appraisement,
Laughing at first and then amazed at my amazement,
That the rose you gave was a gift already cherished,
And the garden whence you plucked it a garden long perished.

But I—I saw that garden, with its one treasure
The tiny mossrose, tiny even by childhood's measure,
And the long morning shadow of the dusty laurel,
And a boy and a girl beneath it, flushed with a childish quarrel.

She wept for her one little bud: but he, outreaching
The hand of brotherly right, would take it for all her beseeching:
And she flung her arms about him, and gave like a sister,
And laughed at her own tears, and wept again when he kissed her.

So the rose is mine long since, and whenever I find it
And drink again the sharp sweet scent of the moss behind it,
I remember the tears of a child, and her love and her laughter,
And the morning shadows of youth and the night that fell thereafter.

Ave, Soror

I LEFT behind the ways of care,
   The crowded hurrying hours,
I breathed again the woodland air,
   I plucked the woodland flowers:

Bluebells as yet but half awake,
   Primroses pale and cool,
Anemones like stars that shake
   In a green twilight pool—

On these still lay the enchanted shade,
   The magic April sun;
With my own child a child I strayed
   And thought the years were one.

As through the copse she went and came
   My senses lost their truth;
I called her by the dear dead name
   That sweetened all my youth.

To a River in the South

CALL me no more, O gentle stream,
To wander through thy sunny dream,
No more to lean at twilight cool
Above thy weir and glimmering pool.

Surely I know thy hoary dawns,
The silver crisp on all thy lawns,
The softly swirling undersong
That rocks thy reeds the winter long.

Surely I know the joys that ring
Through the green deeps of leafy spring;
I know the elfin cups and domes
That are their small and secret homes.

Yet is the light for ever lost
That daily once thy meadows crossed,
The voice no more by thee is heard
That matched the song of stream and bird.

Call me no more!—thy waters roll
Here, in the world that is my soul,
And here, though Earth be drowned in night,
Old love shall dwell with old delight.

The Presentation

WHEN in the womb of Time our souls' own son
Dear love lay sleeping till his natal hour,
Long months I knew not that sweet life begun,
Too dimly treasuring thy touch of power;
     And wandering all those days
      By far-off ways,
Forgot immortal seed must have immortal flower.

Only, beloved, since my beloved thou art
I do remember, now that memory's vain,
How twice or thrice beneath my beating heart
Life quickened suddenly with proudest pain.
  Then dreamed I Love's increase,
  Yet held my peace
Till I might render thee thy own great gift again.

For as with bodies, so with souls it is,
The greater gives, the lesser doth conceive:
That thou hast fathered Love, I tell thee this,
And by my pangs beseech thee to believe.
  Look on his hope divine—
  Thy hope and mine—
Pity his outstretched hands, tenderly him receive!

Amore Altiero

SINCE thou and I have wandered from the highway
 And found with hearts reborn
This swift and unimaginable byway
 Unto the hills of morn,
Shall not our love disdain the unworthy uses
 Of the old time outworn?

I'll not entreat thy half unwilling graces
 With humbly folded palms,
Nor seek to shake thy proud defended places
 With noise of vague alarms,
Nor ask against my fortune's grim pursuing
 The refuge of thy arms.

Thou'lt not withhold for pleasure vain and cruel
 That which has long been mine,
Nor overheap with briefly burning fuel
 A fire of flame divine,
Nor yield the key for life's profaner voices
 To brawl within the shrine.

But thou shalt tell me of thy queenly pleasure
 All that I must fulfil,
And I'll receive from out my royal treasure
 What golden gifts I will,

So that two realms supreme and undisputed
   Shall be one kingdom still.

And our high hearts shall praise the beauty hidden
   In starry-minded scorn
By the same Lord who hath His servants bidden
   To seek with eyes new-born
This swift and unimaginable byway
   Unto the hills of morn.

Against Oblivion

CITIES drowned in olden time
Keep, they say, a magic chime
Rolling up from far below
When the moon-led waters flow.

So within me, ocean deep
Lies a sunken world asleep.
Lest its bells forget to ring,
Memory! set the tide a-swing!

The Inheritance

WHILE I within her secret garden walked,
   The flowers, that in her presence must be dumb,
With me, their fellow-servant, softly talked,
   Attending till the Flower of flowers should come.
Then, since at Court I had arrived but late,
   I was by love made bold
To ask that of my lady's high estate
   I might be told,
And glories of her blood, perpetuate
   In histories old.

Then they, who know the chronicle of Earth,
   Spoke of her loveliness, that like a flame
Far-handed down from noble birth to birth,
   Gladdened the world for ages ere she came.
"Yea, yea," they said, "from Summer's royal sun
   Comes that immortal line,

And was create not for this age alone
    Nor wholly thine,
Being indeed a flower whose root is one
    With Life Divine.

"To the sweet buds that of herself are part
    Already she this portion hath bequeathed,
As, not less surely, into thy proud heart
    Her nobleness, O poet, she hath breathed,
That her inheritance by them and thee
    The world may keep alway,
When the still sunlight of her eyes shall be
    Lost to the day,
And even the fragrance of her memory
    Fading away."

The Pedlar's Song

I TRAMPED among the townward throng
    A sultry summer's morn:
They mocked me loud, they mocked me long,
    They laughed my pack to scorn.
But a likely pedlar holds his peace
    Until the reckoning's told: —
Merrily I to market went, tho' songs were all my gold.

At weary noon I left the town,
    I left the highway straight,
I climbed the silent, sunlit down
    And stood by a castle gate.
Never yet was a house too high
    When the pedlar's heart was bold: —
Merrily I to market went, tho' songs were all my gold.

A lady leaned from her window there
    And asked my wares to see;
Her voice made rich the summer air,
    Richer my soul in me.
She gave me only four little words,
    Words of a language old: —
Merrily I from market came, for all my songs were sold.

An Essay on Criticism

'Tis hard to say if greater waste of time
Is seen in writing or in reading rhyme;
But, of the two, less dangerous it appears
To tire our own than poison others' ears.
Time was, the owner of a peevish tongue,
The pebble of his wrath unheeding flung,
Saw the faint ripples touch the shore and cease,
And in the duckpond all again was peace.
But since that Science on our eyes hath laid
The wondrous clay from her own spittle made,
We see the widening ripples pass beyond,
The pond becomes the world, the world a pond,
All ether trembles when the pebble falls,
And a light word may ring in starry halls.
When first on earth the swift iambic ran
Men here and there were found but nowhere Man.
From whencesoe'er their origin they drew,
Each on its separate soil the species grew,
And by selection, natural or not,
Evolved a fond belief in one small spot.
The Greek himself, with all his wisdom, took
For the wide world his bright Ægean nook,
For fatherland, a town, for public, all
Who at one time could hear the herald bawl:
For him the barbarians beyond his gate
Were lower beings, of a different date;
He never thought on such to spend his rhymes,
And if he did, they never read the *Times*.
Now all is changed, on this side and on that,
The Herald's learned to print and pass the hat;
His tone is so much raised that, far or near,
All with a sou to spend his news may hear,—
And who but, far or near, the sou affords
To learn the worst of foreigners and lords!
So comes the Pressman's heaven on earth, wherein
One touch of hatred proves the whole world kin—
"Our rulers are the best, and theirs the worst,
Our cause is always just and theirs accurst,
Our troops are heroes, hirelings theirs or slaves,
Our diplomats but children, theirs but knaves,
Our Press for independence justly prized,

PLAYING THE GAME

Theirs bought or blind, inspired or subsidized.
For the world's progress what was ever made
Like to our tongue, our Empire and our trade?"
So chant the nations, till at last you'd think
Men could no nearer howl to folly's brink;
Yet some in England lately won renown
By howling word for word, but upside down.

But where, you cry, could poets find a place
(If poets possessed) in this disgrace?
Mails will be Mails, Reviews must be reviews,
But why the Critic with the Bard confuse?
Alas! Apollo, it must be confessed
Has lately gone the way of all the rest.
No more alone upon the far-off hills
With song serene the wilderness he fills,
But in the forum now his art employs
And what he lacks in knowledge gives in noise.
At first, ere he began to feel his feet,
He begged a corner in the hindmost sheet,
Concealed with Answers and Acrostics lay,
And held aloof from Questions of the Day.
But now, grown bold, he dashes to the front,
Among the leaders bears the battle's brunt,
Takes steel in hand, and cheaply unafraid
Spurs a lame Pegasus on Jameson's Raid,
Or pipes the fleet in melodrama's tones.
To ram the Damned on their Infernal Thrones.

Sure, Scriblerus himself could scarce have guessed
The Art of Sinking might be further pressed:
But while these errors almost tragic loom
The Indian Drummer has but raised a boom.
"So well I love my country save that the man
Who serves her can but serve her on my plan;
Be slim, be stalky, leave your Public Schools
To muffs like Bobs and other flannelled fools:
The lordliest life (since Buller made such hay)
Is killing men two thousand yards away;
You shoot the pheasant, but it costs too much
And does not tend to decimate the Dutch;

Your duty plainly then before you stands,
Conscription is the law for seagirt lands;
Prate not of freedom! Since I learned to shoot
I itch to use my ammunition boot."

An odd way this, we thought, to criticize—
This barrackyard "Attention! d— your eyes!"
But England smiled and lightly pardoned him,
For was he not her Mowgli and her Kim?
But now the neighbourhood remonstrance roars,
He's naughty still, and naughty out of doors.
'Tis well enough that he should tell Mamma
Her sons are tired of being what they are,
But to give friendly bears, expecting buns,
A paper full of stale unwholesome Huns—
One might be led to think, from all this work,
That little master's growing quite a Turk.

O Rudyard, Rudyard, in our hours of ease
(Before the war) you were not hard to please:
You loved a regiment whether fore or aft,
You loved a subaltern, however daft,
You loved the very dregs of barrack life,
The amorous colonel and the sergeant's wife.
You sang the land where dawn across the Bay
Comes up to waken queens in Mandalay,
The land where comrades sleep by Cabul ford,
And Valour, brown or white, is Borderlord,
The secret Jungle-life of child and beast,
And all the magic of the dreaming East.
These, these we loved with you, and loved still more
The Seven Seas that break on Britain's shore,
The winds that know her labour and her pride,
And the Long Trail whereon our fathers died.

In that Day's Work be sure you gained, my friend,
If not the critic's name, at least his end;
Your song and story might have roused a slave
To see life bodily and see it brave.
With voice so genial and so long of reach
To your Own People you the Law could preach,

And even now and then without offence
To Lesser Breeds expose their lack of sense.
Return, return! and let us hear again
The ringing engines and the deep-sea rain,
The roaring chanty of the shore-wind's verse,
Too bluff to bicker and too strong to curse.
Let us again with hearts serene behold
The coastwire beacons that we knew of old;
So shall you guide us when the stars are veiled,
And stand among the Lights that never Failed.

Le Byron de Nos Jours; or, The English Bar and Cross Reviewers

STILL must I hear? —while Austin prints his verse
And Satan's sorrows fill Corelli's purse,
Must I not write lest haply some K.C.
To flatter Tennyson should sneer at me?
Or must the Angels of the Darker Ink
No longer tell the public what to think—
Must lectures and reviewing all be stayed
Until they're licensed by the Board of Trade?
Prepare for rhyme—I'll risk it—bite or bark
I'll stop the press for neither Gosse nor Clarke.

O sport most noble, when two cocks engage
With equal blindness and with equal rage!
When each, intent to pick the other's eye,
Sees not the feathers from himself that fly,
And, fired to scorch his rival's every bone,
Ignores the inward heat that grills his own;
Until self-plucked, self-spitted and self-roast,
Each to the other serves himself on toast.

But stay, but stay, you've pitched the key, my Muse,
A semi-tone too low for great Reviews;
Such penny whistling suits the cockpit's hum,
But here's a scene deserves the biggest drum.

Behold where high above the clamorous town
The vast Cathedral-towers in peace look down:
Hark to the entering crowd's incessant tread—
They bring their homage to the mighty dead.

Who in silk gown and fullest-bottomed wig
Approaches yonder, with emotion big?
Room for Sir Edward! now we shall be told
Which shrines are tin, which silver and which gold.
'Tis done! and now by life-long habit bound
He turns to prosecute the crowd around;
Indicts and pleads, sums up the *pro* and *con*,
The verdict finds and puts the black cap on.

"Prisoners, attend! of Queen Victoria's day
I am the Glory, you are the Decay.
You cannot think like Tennyson deceased,
You do not sing like Browning in the least.
Of Tennyson I sanction every word,
Browning I cut to something like one-third:
Though, mind you this, immoral he is not,
Still quite two-thirds I hope will be forgot.
He was to poetry a Tom Carlyle—
And that reminds me, Thomas too was vile.
He wrote a life or two, but parts, I'm sure,
Compared with other parts are very poor.

Now Dickens—most extraordinary—dealt
In fiction with what people really felt.
That proves his genius. Thackeray again
Is so unequal as to cause me pain.
And last of all, with History to conclude,
I've read Macaulay and I've heard of Froude.
That list, with all deductions, Gentlemen,
Will show that 'now' is not the same as 'then':
If you believe the plaintiff you'll declare
That English writers are not what they were."

Down sits Sir Edward with a glowing breast,
And some applause is instantly suppressed.
Now up the nave of that majestic church
A quick uncertain step is heard to lurch.
Who is it? no one knows; but by his mien
He's the head verger, if he's not the Dean.

"What fellow's this that dares to treat us so?
This is no place for lawyers, out you go!
He is a brawler, Sir, who here presumes
To move our laurels and arrange our tombs.
Suppose that Meredith or Stephen said

(Or do you think those gentlemen are dead?)
This age has borne no advocates of rank,
Would not your face in turn be rather blank?
Come now, I beg you, go without a fuss,
And leave these high and heavenly things to us;
You may perhaps be some one, at the Bar,
But you are not in Orders, and we are."

Sir Edward turns to go, but as he wends,
One swift irrelevant retort he sends.
"Your logic and your taste I both disdain,
You've quoted wrong from Jonson and Montaigne."
The shaft goes home, and somewhere in the rear
Birrell in smallest print is heard to cheer.

And yet—and yet—conviction's not complete:
There was a time when Milton walked the street,
And Shakespeare singing in a tavern dark
Would not have much impressed Sir Edward Clarke.
To be alive—ay! there's the damning thing,
For who will buy a bird that's on the wing?
Catch, kill and stuff the creature, once for all,
And he may yet adorn Sir Edward's hall;
But while he's free to go his own wild way
He's not so safe as birds of yesterday.

In fine, if I must choose—although I see
That both are wrong—Great Gosse! I'd rather be
A critic suckled in an age outworn
Than a blind horse that starves knee-deep in corn.

THE POEMS

from **Poems: New and Old, 1912**

April on Waggon Hill

LAD, and can you rest now,
   There beneath your hill?
Your hands are on your breast now,
   But is your heart so still?
'Twas the right death to die, lad,
   A gift without regret
But unless truth's a lie, lad
   You dream of Devon yet.

Ay, ay, the year's awaking,
   The fire's among the ling,
The beechen hedge is breaking,
   The curlew's on the wing;
Primroses are out, lad,
   On the high banks of the Lee,
And the sun stirs the trout, lad,
   From Brendon to the sea.

I know what's in your heart, lad,—
   The mare he used to hunt—
And her blue market-cart, lad,
   With posies tied in front—
We miss them from the moor road,
   They're getting old to roam,
The road they're on's a sure road
   And nearer, lad, to home.

Your name, the name they cherish?
   'Twill fade, lad, 'tis true:
But stone and all may perish
   With little loss to you.
While fame's fame you're Devon, lad,
   The Glory of the West;
Till the roll's called in heaven, lad,
   You may well take your rest.

Songs of the Fleet:

I. Sailing at Dawn

ONE by one the pale stars die before the day now,
    One by one the great ships are stirring from their sleep,
Cables all are rumbling, anchors all a-weigh now,
    Now the fleet's a fleet again, gliding towards the deep.

Now the fleet's a fleet again, bound upon the old ways,
    Splendour of the past comes shining in the spray;
Admirals of old time, bring us on the bold ways!
    Souls of all the sea-dogs, lead the line to-day!

Far away behind us town and tower are dwindling,
    Home becomes a fair dream faded long ago;
Infinitely glorious the height of heaven is kindling,
    Infinitely desolate the shoreless sea below.

Now the fleet's a fleet again, bound upon the old ways,
    Splendour of the past comes shining in the spray;
Admirals of old time, bring us on the bold ways!
    Souls of all the sea-dogs, lead the line to-day!

Once again with proud hearts we make the old surrender,
    Once again with high hearts serve the age to be,
Not for us the warm life of Earth, secure and tender,
    Ours the eternal wandering and warfare of the sea.

Now the fleet's a fleet again, bound upon the old ways,
    Splendour of the past comes shining in the spray;
Admirals of old time, bring us on the bold ways!
    Souls of all the sea-dogs, lead the line to-day!

II. The Song of the Sou' Wester

THE sun was lost in a leaden sky,
    And the shore lay under our lee;
When a great Sou' Wester hurricane high
    Came rollicking up the sea.
He played with the fleet as a boy with boats
    Till out for the Downs we ran,

And he laugh'd with the roar of a thousand throats
  At the militant ways of man:

> *Oh! I am the enemy most of might,*
> *The other be who you please!*
> *Gunner and guns may be all right,*
> *Flags a-flying and armour tight,*
> *But I am the fellow you've first to fight—*
> *The giant that swings the seas.*

A dozen of middies were down below
  Chasing the X they love,
While the table curtseyed long and slow
  And the lamps were giddy above.
The lesson was all of a ship and a shot,
  And some of it may have been true,
But the word they heard and never forgot
  Was the word of the wind that blew:

> *Oh! I am the enemy most of might,*
> *The other be who you please!*
> *Gunner and guns may be all right,*
> *Flags a-flying and armour tight,*
> *But I am the fellow you've first to fight—*
> *The giant that swings the seas.*

The Middy with luck is a Captain soon,
  With luck he may hear one day
His own big guns a-humming the tune
  "'Twas in Trafalgar's Bay."
But wherever he goes, with friends or foes,
  And whatever may there befall,
He'll hear for ever a voice he knows
  For ever defying them all:

> *Oh! I am the enemy most of might,*
> *The other be who you please!*
> *Gunner and guns may be all right,*
> *Flags a-flying and armour tight,*
> *But I am the fellow you've first to fight—*
> *The giant that swings the seas.*

III. The Middle Watch

IN a blue dusk the ship astern
  Uplifts her slender spars,
With golden lights that seem to burn
  Among the silver stars.
Like fleets along a cloudy shore
  The constellations creep,
Like planets on the ocean floor
  Our silent course we keep.

> *And over the endless plain,*
>   *Out of the night forlorn*
> *Rises a faint refrain,*
>   *A song of the day to be born—*
> *Watch, oh watch till ye find again*
>   *Life and the land of morn.*

From a dim West to a dark East
  Our lines unwavering head,
As if their motion long had ceased
  And Time itself were dead.
Vainly we watch the deep below,
  Vainly the void above,
They died a thousand years ago—
  Life and the land we love.

> *But over the endless plain,*
>   *Out of the night forlorn*
> *Rises a faint refrain,*
>   *A song of the day to be born—*
> *Watch, oh watch till ye find again*
>   *Life and the land of morn.*

IV. The Little Admiral

STAND by to reckon up your battleships—
  Ten, twenty, thirty, there they go.
Brag about your cruisers like Leviathans—
  A thousand men a-piece down below.
But here's just one little Admiral—
  We're all of us his brothers and his sons,

And he's worth, O he's worth at the very least
   Double all your tons and all your guns.
        Stand by, etc.

See them on the forebridge signalling—
   A score of men a-hauling hand to hand,
And the whole fleet flying like the wild geese
   Moved by some mysterious command.
Where's the mighty will that shows the way to them,
   The mind that sees ahead so quick and clear?
He's there, Sir, walking all alone there—
   The little man whose voice you never hear.
        Stand by, etc.

There are queer things that only come to sailormen;
   They're true, but they're never understood;
And I know one thing about the Admiral,
   That I can't tell rightly as I should.
I've been with him when hope sank under us—
   He hardly seemed a mortal like the rest,
I could swear that he had stars upon his uniform,
   And one sleeve pinned across his breast.
        Stand by, etc.

Some day we're bound to sight the enemy,
   He's coming, tho' he hasn't yet a name.
Keel to keel and gun to gun he'll challenge us
   To meet him at the Great Armada game.
None knows what may be the end of it,
   But we'll all give our bodies and our souls
To see the little Admiral a-playing him
   A rubber of the old Long Bowls!
        Stand by, etc.

V.   The Song of the Guns at Sea

OH hear! Oh hear!
Across the sullen tide,
Across the echoing dome horizon-wide
What pulse of fear
Beats with tremendous boom?
What call of instant doom,

With thunderstroke of terror and of pride,
With urgency that may not be denied,
Reverberates upon the heart's own drum—
Come! . . . Come! . . . for thou must come!

Come forth, O Soul!
This is thy day of power.
This is thy day and this the glorious hour
That was the goal
Of thy self-conquering strife.
The love of child and wife,
The fields of Earth and the wide ways of Thought—
Did not thy purpose count them all as nought
That in the moment thou thyself mayst give
And in my country's life for ever live?

Therefore rejoice
That in thy passionate prime
Youth's nobler hope disdained the spoils of Time
And thine own choice
Fore-earned for thee this day.
Rejoice! rejoice to obey
In the great hour of life that men call Death
The beat that bids thee draw heroic breath,
Deep-throbbing till thy mortal heart be dumb—
Come! . . . Come! . . . the time is come!

VI. Farewell

MOTHER, with unbowed head
   Hear thou across the sea
The farewell of the dead,
   The dead who died for thee.
Greet them again with tender words and grave,
For, saving thee, themselves they could not save.

To keep the house unharmed
   Their fathers built so fair,
Deeming endurance armed
   Better than brute despair,
They found the secret of the word that saith,
"Service is sweet, for all true life is death."

So greet thou well thy dead
   Across the homeless sea,
And be thou comforted
   Because they died for thee.
Far off they served, but now their deed is done
For evermore their life and thine are one.

Rilloby-Rill

GRASSHOPPERS four a-fiddling went,
      Heigh ho! never be still!
They earned but little towards their rent,
But all day long with their elbows bent
      They fiddled a tune called Rilloby-rilloby,
      Fiddled a tune called Rilloby-rill.

Grasshoppers soon on Fairies came,
      Heigh ho! never be still!
Fairies asked with a manner of blame,
"Where do you come from, what is your name?
      What do you want with your Rilloby-rilloby,
      What do you want with your Rilloby-rill?"

"Madam, you see me before you stand,
      Heigh ho! never be still!
The Old Original Favourite Grand
Grasshopper's Green Herbarian Band,
      And the tune we play is Rilloby-rilloby
      Madam, the tune is Rilloby-rill."

Fairies hadn't a word to say,
      Heigh ho! never be still!
Fairies seldom are sweet by day,
But the Grasshoppers merrily fiddled away,
      O but they played with a willoby-rilloby,
      O but they played with a willoby-will!

Fairies slumber and sulk at noon,
      Heigh ho! never be still!
But at last the kind old motherly moon
Brought them dew in a silver spoon,
      And they turned to ask for a Rilloby-rilloby,
      One more round of Rilloby-rill.

Ah! but nobody now replied,
    Heigh ho! never be still!
When day went down the music died,
Grasshoppers four lay side by side,
      And there was an end of their Rilloby-rilloby,
      There was an end of their Rilloby-rill.

THE POEMS

from St. George's Day and Other Poems, 1918

The War Films

O LIVING pictures of the dead,
    O songs without a sound,
O fellowship whose phantom tread
    Hallows a phantom ground—
How in a gleam have these revealed
    The faith we had not found.

We have sought God in a cloudy Heaven,
    We have passed by God on earth:
His seven sins and his sorrows seven,
    His wayworn mood and mirth,
Like a ragged doll have hid from us
    The secret of his birth.

Brother of men, when now I see
    The lads go forth in line,
Thou knowest my heart is hungry in me
    As for thy bread and wine:
Thou knowest my heart is bowed in me
    To take their death for mine.

St. George's Day

    YPRES, 1915

TO fill the gap, to bear the brunt
    With bayonet and with spade,
Four hundred to a four-mile front
    Unbacked and undismayed—
What men are these, of what great race,
    From what old shire or town,
That run with such goodwill to face
    Death on a Flemish down?

Let be! they bind a broken line:
  As men die, so die they.
Land of the free! their life was thine,
  It is St. George's Day.

Yet say whose ardour bids them stand
  At bay by yonder bank,
Where a boy's voice and a boy's hand
  Close up the quivering rank.
Who under those all-shattering skies
  Plays out his captain's part
With the last darkness in his eyes
  And *Domum* in his heart?

Let be, let be! in yonder line
  All names are burned away.
Land of his love! the fame be thine,
  It is St. George's Day.

Hic Jacet

QUI IN HOC SAECULO FIDELITER MILITAVIT

HE that has left hereunder
  The signs of his release
Feared not the battle's thunder
  Nor hoped that wars should cease;
No hatred set asunder
  His warfare from his peace.

Nor feared he in his sleeping
  To dream his work undone,
To hear the heathen sweeping
  Over the lands he has won;
For he has left in keeping
  His sword unto his son.

The King's Highway

WHEN moonlight flecks the cruiser's decks
    And engines rumble slow,
When Drake's own star is bright above
    And Time has gone below,
They may hear who list the far-off sound
    Of a long-dead never-dead mirth,
In the mid watch still they may hear who will
    The Song of the Larboard Berth.

In a dandy frigate or a well-found brig,
    In a sloop or a seventy-four,
In a great Firstrate with an Admiral's flag
    And a hundred guns or more,
In a fair light air, in a dead foul wind,
    At midnight or midday,
Till the good ship sink her mids shall drink
    To the King and the King's Highway!

The mids they hear—no fear, no fear!
    They know their own ship's ghost:
Their young blood beats to the same old song
    And roars to the same old toast.
So long as the sea-wind blows unbound
    And the sea-wave breaks in spray,
For the Island's sons the word still runs—
    "The King, and the King's Highway!"

A Chanty of the Emden

THE captain of the *Emden*
   He spread his wireless net,
And told the honest British tramp
   Where raiders might be met:
Where raiders might be met, my lads,
   And where the coast was clear,
And there he sat like a crafty cat
   And sang while they drew near—
     "Now you come along with me, sirs,
       You come along with me!
      You've had your run, old England's done,
        And it's time you were home from sea!"

The seamen of old England
   They doubted his intent,
And when he hailed, "Abandon ship!"
   They asked him what he meant:
They asked what he meant, my lads,
   The pirate and his crew,
But he said, "Stand by! your ship must die,
   And it's luck you don't die too!
     So you come along with me, sirs,
       You come along with me:
      We find our fun now yours is done,
        And it's time you were home from sea!"

He took her, tramp or trader,
   He sank her like a rock,
He stole her coal and sent her down
   To Davy's deep-sea dock:
To Davy's deep-sea dock, my lads,
   The finest craft afloat,
And as she went he still would sing
   From the deck of his damned old boat—
     "Now you come along with me, sirs,
       You come along with me:
      Your good ship's done with wind and sun,
        And it's time you were home from sea!"

The captain of the *Sydney*
   He got the word by chance;
Says he, "By all the Southern Stars,
   We'll make the pirates dance:
We'll make the pirates dance, my lads,
   That this mad work have made,
For no man knows how a hornpipe goes
   Until the music's played.
      So you come with me, sirs,
         You come along with me:
      The game's not won till the rubber's done,
         And it's time to be home from sea!"

The *Sydney* and the *Emden*
   They went it shovel and tongs,
The *Emden* had her rights to prove,
   The *Sydney* had her wrongs:
The *Sydney* had her wrongs, my lads,
   And a crew of South Sea blues;
Their hearts were hot, and as they shot
   They sang like kangaroos—
      "Now you come along with me, sirs,
         You come along with me:
      You've had your fun, you ruddy old Hun,
         And it's time you were home from sea!"

The *Sydney* she was straddled,
   But the *Emden* she was strafed,
They knocked her guns and funnels out,
   They fired her fore and aft:
They fired her fore and aft, my lads,
   And while the beggar burned
They salved her crew to a tune they knew,
   But never had rightly learned—
      "Now you come along with me, sirs,
         You come along with me:
      We'll find you fun till the fighting's done
         And the pirate's off the sea—
      Till the pirate's off the sea, my lads,
         Till the pirate's off the sea:
      We'll find them fun till the fighting's done
         And the pirate's off the sea!"

The Toy Band

A SONG OF THE GREAT RETREAT

DREARY lay the long road, dreary lay the town,
    Lights out and never a glint o' moon:
Weary lay the stragglers, half a thousand down,
    Sad sighed the weary big Dragoon.
"Oh! if I'd a drum here to make them take the road again,
    Oh! if I'd a fife to wheedle, Come, boys, come!
You that mean to fight it out, wake and take your load again,
    Fall in! Fall in! Follow the fife and drum!

"Hey, but here's a toy shop, here's a drum for me,
    Penny whistles too to play the tune!
Half a thousand dead men soon shall hear and see
    We're a band!" said the weary big Dragoon.
"Rubadub! Rubadub! Wake and take the road again,
    Wheedle-deedle-deedle-dee, Come, boys, come!
You that mean to fight it out, wake and take your load again,
    Fall in! Fall in! Follow the fife and drum!"

Cheerly goes the dark road, cheerly goes the night,
    Cheerly goes the blood to keep the beat:
Half a thousand dead men marching on to fight
    With a little penny drum to lift their feet.
Rubadub! Rubadub! Wake and take the road again,
    Wheedle-deedle-deedle-dee, Come, boys, come!
You that mean to fight it out, wake and take your load again,
    Fall in! Fall in! Follow the fife and drum!

As long as there's an Englishman to ask a tale of me,
    As long as I can tell the tale aright,
We'll not forget the penny whistle's wheedle-deedle-dee
    And the big Dragoon a-beating down the night,
Rubadub! Rubadub! Wake and take the road again,
    Wheedle-deedle-deedle-dee, Come, boys, come!
You that mean to fight it out, wake and take your load again,
    Fall in! Fall in! Follow the fife and drum!

A Letter from the Front

I WAS out early to-day, spying about
From the top of a haystack—such a lovely morning—
And when I mounted again to canter back
I saw across a field in the broad sunlight
A young gunner subaltern, stalking along
With a rook-rifle held at the ready and—would you believe it?—
A domestic cat, soberly marching behind him.

So I laughed, and felt quite well-disposed to the youngster,
And shouted out "The top of the morning" to him,
And wished him "Good sport!" —and then I remembered
My rank, and his, and what I ought to be doing;
And I rode nearer, and added, "I can only suppose
You have not seen the Commander-in-Chief's orders
Forbidding English officers to annoy their Allies
By hunting and shooting."
      But he stood and saluted
And said earnestly, "I beg your pardon, sir,
I was only going out to shoot a sparrow
To feed my cat with."

      So there was the whole picture—
The lovely early morning, the occasional shell
Screeching and scattering past us, the empty landscape—
Empty, except for the young gunner saluting
And the cat, anxiously watching his every movement.

I may be wrong, and I may have told it badly,
But it struck *me* as being extremely ludicrous.

from A Perpetual Memory and Other Poems, 1939

The Great Memory

> *NOBIS cum pereant amorum*
> *Et dulcedines et decor,*
> *Tu nostrorum praeteritorum,*
> *Anima mundi, sis memor.*

ON the mind's lonely hill-top lying
   I saw man's life go by like a breath,
And Love that longs to be love undying,
   Bowed with fear of the void of death.
"If Time be master," I heard her weeping,
   "How shall I save the loves I bore?
They are gone, they are gone beyond my keeping—
   Anima mundi, sis memor!

"Soul of the World, thou seest them failing—
   Childhood's loveliness, child's delight—
Lost as stars in the daylight paling,
   Trodden to earth as flowers in fight.
Surely in these thou hast thy pleasure—
   Yea! they are thine and born therefor:
Shall they not be with thy hid treasure? —
   Anima mundi, sis memor!

"Only a moment we can fold them
   Here in the home whose life they are:
Only a moment more behold them
   As in a picture, small and far.
Oh, in the years when even this seeming
   Lightens the eyes of Love no more,
Dream them still in thy timeless dreaming
   Anima mundi, sis memor!"

March 5, 1921

ME at the dawn's first breath
   Thee in the dusk of death
   Thy love and my love tended:
We shall be mother and son
After all days are done
   All darkness ended.

The Linnet's Nest

O WHAT has wrought again the miracle of Spring?
This old garden of mine that was so beautiful
And died so utterly—what power of earth or sky
From dead sticks and dead mould has raised up Paradise?

The flow'rs we knew we welcome again in their turns—
Primrose, anemone, daffodil and tulip,
Blossom of cherry, blossom of pear and apple,
Iris and columbine, and now the white cistus.

In a round bush it grows, this cistus of delight,
A mound of delicate pure white crinkled petals,
In the heart of the garden, where the green paths cross,
Where the old stone dial throws its morning shadow.

Come nearer, and speak low; watch while I put aside
This thickly flow'ring spray, and stoop till you can see
There in the shadowy centre, a tiny nest,
And on it, facing us, a bright-eyed bird sitting.

She has five eggs, shaped and speckled most daintily;
But this she cannot know, nor how they are quick'ning
With that which soon will be on the wing, and singing
The ancestral linnet-song of thoughtless rapture.

No, this she cannot know, nor indeed anything
That we call knowledge, nor such love and hope as ours:
Yet she for her treasure will endure and tremble,
And so find peace that passeth our understanding.

You wonder at my wonder—the bird has instinct,
The law by dust ordained for that which dust creates?
What then is beauty? and love? my heart is restless
To know what love and beauty are worth in the end.

The bird I know will fly; nest, blood, cistus, garden
Will all be lost when winter takes the world again:
Yet in my mind their loveliness will still survive
Till I too in my turn obey the laws of dust.

Are we then all? Is there no Life in whom our nests,
Our trembling hopes and unintelligent loves
May still, for the beauty they had, the faith they kept,
Live on as in a vast eternal memory?

Yet so for us would beauty still be meaningless,
Mortal and meaningless—our hearts are restless still
To be one with that spirit from whom all life springs,
And therein to behold all beauty for ever.

Perhaps the linnet too is more than dust: perhaps
She, though so small, of so quick-perishing beauty,
Is none the less a part of His immortal dream
And beneath her breast cherishes the divine life.

The Nightjar

WE loved our Nightjar, but she would not stay with us.
We had found her lying as dead, but soft and warm,
Under the apple tree beside the old thatched wall.
Two days we kept her in a basket by the fire,
Fed her, and thought she well might live—till suddenly
In the very moment of most confiding hope
She raised herself all tense, quivered and drooped and died.
Tears sprang into my eyes—why not? the heart of man
Soon sets itself to love a living companion,
The more so if by chance it asks some care of him.
And this one had the kind of loveliness that goes
Far deeper than the optic nerve—full fathom five
To the soul's ocean cave, where Wonder and Reason
Tell their alternate dreams of how the world was made.
So wonderful she was—her wings the wings of night
But powdered here and there with tiny golden clouds
And wave-line markings like sea-ripples on the sand.
O how I wish I might never forget that bird—
Never!
        But even now, like all beauty of earth,
She is fading from me into the dusk of Time.

The Star in the West

LISTEN with me tonight, listen O tenderly
To the wordless wailing of yonder newborn Child.
In vain his mother's arms enfold him and soothe him,
In vain her voice murmurs the song of tireless love.

Why does he weep? Why will he not be comforted?
Here on the threshold of his life, what does he dread?
Is it the dimness of the stable where he lies,
Or the gaunt ox and ass, shadows of toil to come?

Presently will he not uplift his wond'ring eyes
To see the face that is to be his earthly rest?
Will not the shining star above his low roof stayed
Lighten his childish dream with serene rays of peace?

Dare not ask! —unless ye dare also to hear
The story of his cross, his first and second death—
That men have murdered Night, and made stars of their own,
And flung them down from heav'n, and Peace has died by fire.

A Perpetual Memory

GOOD FRIDAY, 1915

BROKEN and pierced, hung on the bitter wire,
   By their most precious death the Sons of Man
Redeem for us the life of our desire—
   O Christ how often since the world began!

To Christopher

(FOR HIS WEDDING DAY)

YOUNG lover, for us that knew
      You as a boy
Your parents, and theirs too,
      And all the joy
That in their line so long
      Has descended,

Life to-day soars up as a song
         That is still unended.

We are old, young love, our bones
         Ache by the way,
Our feet are slow on the stones,
         Our twilight's grey,
But you, you have given us again
         Memory and trust:
We are older than Age, we are stronger than pain,
         We are more than our dust.

A Letter to R.B. after a Visit

AUGUST, 1921
(WRITTEN IN HIS HOST'S "NEW NARRATVE METHOD")

MY dear Bridges before I do anything else
I must thank you for my visit: it was all good—
From the kind welcome and renewal of friendship
Down to that excellent wine and Devonshire cream.
I believe I did say something of my feelings,
But words are useless: I might go on heaping them
Epithet on epithet all down my paper
Like the elephant piling teak in Kipling's poem
And still leave the real thing wholly unexpressed.
But I do wish I could give you some idea
Of how much I like your new narrative method
And admire the poems by which you shew it off,
Especially of course the polyglot parrot
Who demonstrates in a ludicrous but apt image
How you in verse whose service is perfect freedom
Can tell a plain prosy tale, or write a letter,
Or toss a song to the stars or the salt seawind,
Or toll the deep old Latin and Italian bells,
Or dance among French accents without breaking them
Or wake again the poignant memories of Greece.
But here is post time, and this must go.
                        Believe me
My dear Bridges (how glad I am to write the words)
If you are my "old friend," as your kindness declared,
I am yours too, as always grateful and devoted.
                                                H.N.

Cricket

OUR countrymen of England who winter here at ease
And send abroad their cricketers to fight across the seas—
They long to win the rubber, but inwardly they know
    The game's the game: howe'er the luck may go.

They know the English skipper may cry "a head! a head!"
And t'other like a Kangaroo may toss a tail instead,
But cricketers can smile away the force of Fortune's blow
    For a man's a man: howe'er the luck may go.

To field upon a field of brick, to bowl beneath the blaze,
To bat and bat and bat and bat for days and days and days,
And then to lose—there's something wrong— but no! but no!
                                                   but no!
    The game's the game: howe'er the luck may go.

All men alive are cricketers, and stand to face the odds,
And some will trust in cunning tricks, and some in heathen gods:
But you my son were born and bred where what I say is so—
    The game's the game: howe'er the luck may go.

Epitaph on a Public Man

STRANGER if you desire to know
What End was his who lies below,
In far too many Chairs he sat
And died worn out by merely that.

The Old to the Young

NOW, dear child, when childhood ends,
Comes the time to weed your friends:
Not of course that they'll be told
They're too dowdy dull or old
But we must admit the truth
Life is short and youth is youth.
Half must go in any case
Topsy turvy into space,
That the rest, the happier few

Still may walk and talk with you.
Then may this old house be heard
Kindly, if it breathe a word:
If it beg, since here you were
As beloved as you were fair,
You'll revisit still at times
These old rooms and lawns and limes,
These old people, her and him,
Till their memories are dim,
Till you too are moving West
Far from any last year's nest.

Poet's Epitaph

WHAT I was and yet shall be
You have seen and could not see.
Say then only "Here below
Lies a Worm without his Glow."

APPENDIX A

NOTES

Admirals All – Charles Howard, 2nd Baron Howard of Effingham (1536–1624), known as Howard of Effingham, was commander of the English forces during the Spanish Armada and was chiefly responsible for the victory. Sir Richard Grenville (1542–1591) was an English privateer who was part of the repulse of the Spanish Armada. He died at the Battle of Flores in 1591 in which his bravery allowed other ships to escape. Vice Admiral John Benbow (1653–1702) fought against France during the Nine Years' War (1688–1697) and the War of the Spanish Succession (1701–1714) due to which he achieved national fame. Vice Admiral Cuthbert Collingwood, 1st Baron Collingwood (1748–1810) was an admiral of the Royal Navy, notable as a partner with Lord Nelson in several of the British victories of the Napoleonic Wars, and frequently as Nelson's successor in commands – see 'Northumberland' below. Vice Admiral John Byron (1723–1786) was governor of Newfoundland and circumnavigated the world as a commodore with his own squadron in 1764–1766. He fought in battles in the Seven Years' War and the American Revolution and was grandfather of the poet Lord Byron. Robert Devereux, 2nd Earl of Essex (circa 1565–1601), was an English nobleman and a favourite of Queen Elizabeth I. In 1596 he distinguished himself by the capture of Cadiz. Admiral George Brydges Rodney, 1st Baron Rodney, KB (1718 –1792), was a British naval officer. He is best known for his commands in the American War of Independence, particularly his victory over the French at the Battle of the Saintes in 1782. For Blake, see the note on 'The Death of Admiral Blake' below.

San Stefano – The *HMS Menelaus*, the subject of the poem, was a fifth-rate frigate launched in 1810 under the command of Captain Peter Parker. Parker came from a long line of distinguished naval men; he was the son of Admiral Christopher Parker, grandson of Admiral Sir Peter Parker (friend of Nelson) and great-grandson of Admiral Sir William Parker. He was also a grandson of Admiral Byron and a cousin of Lord Byron, the poet. Under Parker, the ship saw action as part of the blockade of Toulon in 1812 and was also instrumental in making raids of the Maryland coast. It was here that Parker was killed at the Battle of Caulk's Field on 31 August 1814. A year after that the *Menelaus* was part of a convoy which captured a number of French vessels, one of the last actions of the Napoleonic Wars. Following an initial burial in Bermuda, Parker's body was returned to be interred with his relations in St. Margaret's, Westminster. In later years the *Menelaus* served as a hospital ship before being broken up in 1897.

Drake's Drum – On 3 January 1896 Kaiser Wilhelm II sent a message to Paul Kruger, President of the Transvaal Republic, congratulating him on repelling the Jameson Raid which had been an ill-fated attempt to stimulate anti-Boer feeling and act as the precursor to a rebellion by the British expatriate miners. The Kaiser also ordered a party of marines to proceed to Pretoria on the pretext of protecting the German community there. In response to this potentially threatening move, Britain dispatched a Special Service Squadron to be on standby. Newbolt's poem was conceived as a response to these events and, two weeks after its completion, he sent it to Sidney Low, editor of *The St. James's Gazette*. It appeared on 15 January and immediately caught the public mood. Low reversed the order of verses one and two, the form in which it appears today. The drum referred to in the title is preserved in Buckland Abbey, the Drake family seat in Devon where, legend has it, it is supposed to sound whenever England is in danger.

Hawke – Edward Hawke, 1st Baron Hawke (1705–1781) was a naval commander celebrated for his victory over the French at the Battle of Quiberon Bay in November 1759 during the Seven Years' War. His decisive triumph, celebrated here by Newbolt, prevented a French invasion of England, and put the French fleet out of action for the remainder of the war. Later, Hawke became First Lord of the Admiralty (1766–1771).

The Fighting Téméraire – The *HMS Temeraire* was a ship of the line launched in 1798 and which took part in the French Revolutionary and Napoleonic Wars. After a period with the Channel Fleet, she joined Nelson's blockade of the Franco-Spanish fleet in Cadiz in 1805, before serving alongside him at Trafalgar. Such was her bravery in coming to the rescue of the flagship *Victory*, as well as in capturing two French vessels, that she achieved national renown. Later in the war she was used as part of the blockade of French fleets off the Spanish coast and participated in defending convoys from Danish gunboat attacks. Laid up from 1813, she was variously a prison ship, a victualling depot, and a guard ship before being sold and broken up in 1838. Turner's famous painting (which hangs in the National Gallery, London) painted in 1839 depicts her final journey and is, amongst other things, symbolic of the demise of Britain's unquestioned power and control in the world. The last two stanzas of Newbolt's poem allude to Turner's painting: '*Now the sunset's breezes shiver* […] *And she's fading down the river*'.

Vitaï Lampada – The title translates as 'Torch of Life' and comes from Lucretius' *De Rereum Natura*. It appears that Newbolt lifted the phrase exactly from Book II, line 79, although he added the umlaut, presumably to influence the pronunciation. Due to its continuing popularity, the poem remained a source of frustration for Newbolt. Even as late as 1916 he was to write how 'in Plymouth it is reported that Drake's Drum has been heard! Write me down an Ass, if you will, or a dullard, or an Aggravating Argumentative Ambècile [sic], but remember to add that I did give my Country a Legend of real value. You needn't add that I also gave it the phrase "play the game" – I find even blighted foreigners now using it. If it *must* go down to my credit, I hope that Posterity won't take it for my idea of Poetry! as "to be or not to be, that is the question" is commonly supposed to be W.S.'s' (Newbolt, letter to Alice Hylton, 17 March 1916, quoted in Margaret Newbolt, 1942: 224).

He Fell Among Thieves – In a rare instance of Newbolt not being strictly accurate with the facts, the basis of this poem was indeed the story of the adventurer and soldier Lieutenant George Hayward who was killed in the region of India which is now Pakistan in July 1870. Subsequent research, however, by former Viceroy of India Lord Curzon (who hugely admired the work) found that it was unlikely that a young lieutenant would have had the Oxbridge education suggested in the poem – College Eight, Dons, and so on. The model for this poem may well, therefore, have been a combination of Newbolt himself and his friend Francis Younghusband.

Ionicus – The subject of this poem is William Johnson Cory (1823–1892), an English educator, classical scholar, and poet. Dismissed from his teaching post at Eton in 1872 following the discovery of an indiscreet letter written to one of his pupils, Cory later settled in London where he taught the Classics to a number of adult learners including Margaret Newbolt. In the years since, suspicion has fallen on Cory as possibly having engaged in sexual relationships with his younger students, although this is unsubstantiated. None of this would have been known by Newbolt, although 'his life a tangle seemed' may be a subtle reference to Cory's homosexuality which was then illegal. Cory was known to stop teaching if soldiers were parading close by so he and his pupils could observe them. Sir Denis Pack was an Irish soldier who distinguished himself in the Peninsular War and commanded a brigade of Picton's Division at Quatre Bras and Waterloo. Sir Thomas Picton had an equally distinguished military career in the West Indies and Spain before coming out of retirement to fight at the Battle of Waterloo. His last words were reputedly 'Charge! Charge! Hurrah!', before he was struck down by a cannonball.

Minora Sidera – At the time of writing, the DNB (*Dictionary of National Biography*) was being edited by Newbolt's friend Leslie Stephen, better known today for being the father of the novelist Virginia Woolf and the painter Vanessa Bell. In a biography of Stephen, Frederic William Maitland (1906) recalls his daughters telling the story of their father walking around the house and Kensington Gardens reciting Newbolt's 'Admirals All'.

The Vigil – As with other poems by Newbolt which had originally been written for the Boer War, 'The Vigil' was re-printed on 5 August 1914, the first day of the First World War. According to one academic, 'it sold so many copies, and was thought to have had such a great effect on national morale, that he [Newbolt] was given a knighthood' (Girouard, 1981: 283).

Admiral Death – Although written with the swaying rhythm of the rollicking sea shanty, the key to this poem lies in its fine juxtaposition of this mood with the omniscient presence of the spirit of death, an ever-present danger for sailors. According to Newbolt's memoirs, the inspiration for the poem was a sitting for the Scottish artist William Strang (1859–1921), best known today for his portrait of Vita Sackville-West complete with a red hat. As Newbolt remembered: 'While I sat to him he set up an oil picture for me to fix my eyes upon- it was a Holbeinesque thing with a jigging skeleton in it, and he said as he drew me, "You should do a ballad on Death - Admiral Death". I asked for a clearer indication of his idea: under pressure he tried to give it - in a sentence or two which afforded me no kind of illumination. But afterwards - in less than a week - the ballad came to me suddenly and easily with a meaning of my own' (Newbolt, 1932: 212).

Messmates – The haunting mood captured here showcases a too often under-appreciated facet of Newbolt's poetry. In exploring this aspect Herbert Palmer was moved to write of 'Messmates' that 'he seemed to reach the high-water of that kind of thing, though the poem is also important for another reason, for it is written in a very original metre, one that seems to have no precedent' (Palmer, 1938: 42).

The Death of Admiral Blake – One of the greatest naval men, General at Sea Robert Blake (1598–1657) is widely recognized for being the founder of Britain's supremacy on the seas through his dynamic leadership and skills of organization. Commanding Parliamentary and Cromwellian fleets during the First Anglo-Dutch War and the Anglo-Spanish War, Blake died of old wounds within sight of Plymouth. The poem concerns this last return and his desire to see the Somerset landscapes of his youth before he dies. As is the case with 'He Fell Among Thieves' not only does the protagonist reflect on the things dear to him, but also how these shaped the man he is today. Newbolt thus combines two forms of patriotism – that of serving one's country through deed but also love of country through appreciation of the beauty found within her landscapes.

The Non-Combatant – The origins of this poem lie in a less than sympathetic review of *Admirals All*, published in January 1898 in *The Athenaeum*. In it, the point was made that not only was the triumphant reception afforded to the book reflective of the poor taste of the reading public but also that patriotism was not itself a fit subject for poetry: 'Patriotism, an excellent virtue in a citizen, is to a poet a somewhat dangerous master … if a poem about war is to be really a poem, war, certainly, must be treated in the grand manner and with sufficient intellectual remoteness. The moment you become a partisan you cease to be a poet' (*The Athenaeum*, 22 January 1898: 111). The outraged Newbolt composed in reply both a letter and this poem. Whilst he judiciously withdrew the letter from publication fearing it was too controversial, the poem was substituted as a response. In it, Newbolt expresses his view that whilst the poet might be 'born to fail,/ A name without an echo' he nevertheless has a role to play both in fulfilling 'the ancestral rites' and keeping alive 'The eternal fire' but also in handing on knowledge of the past to future generations.

Clifton Chapel – This occupies a seminal position in Newbolt's *oeuvre*. It perfectly articulates his ideas around chivalry as a young boy about to start at Clifton is shown the school chapel by his father, a place where he learned the values he now seeks to live by and which he here outlines to his son. Although 'yonder brass' does not exist in real life, Newbolt nonetheless provided a translation of the Latin: '"Who far from here,/ Who before his time, died,/ But a soldier, but for his country."' As with other poems about Clifton, Newbolt puts forth the idea that school is a 'microcosm of life' (Winterbottom, 1986: 44).

The Echo – Harry Plunket Greene (1865–1936) was an Irish baritone who became famous for his concert and oratorio repertoire. As a friend of Elgar's, he was the original baritone in *The Dream of Gerontius*. He was an exact contemporary of Newbolt at Clifton. Published first in *The Cliftonian*, the poem was subsequently set to music by the music master Arthur Peppin and was sung by Greene.

Fidele's Grassy Tomb – As noted in the Introduction, this was a poem inspired by a talk given by a local historian about a legend surrounding the church at Orchardleigh. First published in *The Spectator* in February 1898, its title was taken from a 1744 poem by William Collins, which begins, 'To fair Fidele's grassy tomb'. Fidele was the name used by Imogen when in disguise in Shakespeare's play *Cymbeline*. Combining the two aspects lead to Newbolt elaborating the story and, in his preferred ballad form, putting forth the importance of the twin virtues of loyalty (fidelity) and resolve.

Imogen – The girl dancing in the poem is Imogen Booth, a friend of Newbolt's daughter Celia. Here she is about 14.

The Invasion – Newbolt's interest in chivalry and the glory of the past finds strong expression here. In his novels *The Old Country* and *Aladore*, as well as in his retelling of Froissart's *Chronicles*, he consciously used the past as a model for the present. 'The Invasion' suggests aspects of 'Merrie England', which, although nostalgic, also carry a hint of menace, hence its popularity at the beginning of the First World War.

Ireland, Ireland – Demands for Irish Home Rule and even independence had been growing since the 1860s. The situation came to a head, however, with Gladstone's failed attempts to introduce successive Home Rule

APPENDIX A

Bills. The Irish Government Bill of 1893 passed the Commons but was defeated in the Conservative-majority House of Lords. Following that, the Local Government (Ireland) Act of 1898 enfranchised local electors thereby giving a renewed impetus to calls for independence. This poem, first published in *The Saturday Review* on 17 September 1898, seems to be offering support to the cause and, although an imitation of the early faery music of Yeats, was well received by the reviewers: '"Ireland, Ireland" which though of but three verses has a high quality' (*The Edinburgh Review*, Vol. 210 (Oct. 1909): 397).

Moonset – This poem was inspired by a long journey Newbolt made from Orchardleigh in Somerset to Northumberland in order to visit his friend Dr. Thomas Hodgkin, the historian. Its origins are recollected in his own autobiography: 'My last visit to Bamburgh was in the winter of 1898. I left Orchardleigh and its Christmas Party in the early dawn of the 6th of January and was driven to Frome Station just when the full moon was setting behind the gaunt woods by which we had to pass. She had a strange unearthly light - golden instead of silver - and looked like a huge yellow lantern lit for some festivity of celestial giants. I felt awed and spellbound and the time seemed endlessly long until we escaped from the park and out on to the open high road. An hour or two of my day's journey was spent in "recollecting in tranquillity" this strange experience of "Moonset"' (Newbolt, 1932: 233). Vanessa Jackson has described it equally affectionately: 'the appeal of the poem lies in its direct, light language and almost conversational tone – indeed in its simplicity' (Jackson, 1994: 117).

The Sailing of the Long-Ships – Although concerned with the embarkation of soldiers to South Africa, a longship could also refer to those vessels used successfully by the Vikings.

Waggon Hill – The Battle of Wagon Hill took place during the Siege of Ladysmith in South Africa on 6 January 1900. The town was garrisoned by the British and besieged by the Boers. Despite the Boers attacking throughout the day, they were eventually forced to retreat following a bayonet charge in the rain from the 1st Devonshire Regiment. Newbolt's poem thus is a celebration of their bravery, which he compares to that of Sir Francis Drake, a famous son of the county.

The Volunteer – First printed in *The Spectator* on 9 December 1899, this short piece about a schoolboy soldier was highly regarded at the time of its publication: 'The best poem which the war has yet produced ... has, indeed, a simplicity and sincerity which lift I above occasional poetry to a plane of permanence' (*The Academy*, 16 December 1899: 712).

The Schoolfellow – This poem concerns a former captain of the school football team who has gone to fight in the Boer War. First printed in *The Spectator* on 18 November 1899.

The Only Son – Once again on the theme of commemoration, here Newbolt imagines parents mourning their dead soldier son. Despite being constructed as a ballad, the choice of form in this case manages to elevate its sentiments.

The School at War – Written in May 1901 and a poem tying together two of Newbolt's key interests – patriotic warfare, and the role of schools in preparing their pupils to fight through the development of courage and *esprit de corps*.

Commemoration – Written in July 1901, a week after the annual celebrations at Clifton where a long list of those who had been killed in the Boer War was read out. 'As the casualty list lengthened a large number of Old Cliftonians came together in the summer of 1901 to discuss the question of a Memorial. The Chairman was that white-haired Patriarch of the Clifton world, John Percival, now a Bishop. He chaired the Committee elected to arrange for a Memorial and among the ten O.C. members were Henry Newbolt and his school contemporaries Rowland Whitehead and John McTaggert' (Winterbottom, 1986: 54). The memorial was formally unveiled at Commemoration in 1904 by Lord Methuen.

Outward Bound – Newbolt had earlier composed a poem entitled 'Homeward Bound' (not included in the current selection) which described a sailor heading home and in which England was invoked as a land of ancient history – 'home of all our mortal dream'. Although written and published later, 'Outward Bound' serves as a companion piece in which the same sailor exhibits his reluctance to once again leave that land and become a 'son in exile'. Newbolt hugely admired the poetry of Robert Browning and the contrasting situations of these poems mirror Browning's own 'Meeting at Night' and 'Parting at Morning' as well as suggesting subtle echoes of the famous 'Home Thoughts from Aboard'.

APPENDIX A

From Generation to Generation – Indicative of a mood that would be more fully developed in subsequent collections, the addressee of this poem is Newbolt's 9-year-old son Francis. It was written only a few months before peace was signed and suggests the sadness and horror that the Boer War had unleashed and which, Newbolt hoped, would not be repeated.

When I Remember – According to Vanessa Jackson, 'Newbolt wrote this poem in October 1899, soon after his tenth wedding anniversary. He originally entitled it simply, "To My Wife"' (Jackson, 1994: 120).

Yattendon – Yattendon is a small village in Berkshire where the Poet Laureate and close friend to Newbolt, Robert Bridges, lived. It was in his house that Newbolt first presented him with 'Drake's Drum', the poem which was to make his name and subsequent reputation. 'The pilgrim world must come' refers, therefore, not simply to Newbolt's own visits but the high esteem in which he held Bridges.

Northumberland – The remote county held a special place for Newbolt and he was a frequent visitor. His friends there included Sir Andrew Noble who lived at Chillingham Castle, Howard Pease who lived at Otterburn, Thomas Hodgkin whose house was in Bamburgh (see 'Moonset'), and Sir Edward Grey who was Member of Parliament for Berwick-upon-Tweed. The fact that one of Newbolt's military heroes, Vice Admiral Cuthbert Collingwood, hailed from the county, as well as the strong connection between the local regiment and the Percy family, may also perhaps have inspired Newbolt.

Sacrementum Supremum – The title translates to 'the last sacrament' and is entirely appropriate given the way in which the poem appears to be an offering of thanks for those whose chivalry and courage ('Life is no life to him that dares not die') have seen them bonded together in battle. The fact that their 'last rites' are a paean to chivalric virtues is a typical Newbolt flourish.

Ave, Soror – Composed in Hursely Copse near Winchester and with a title meaning 'Farewell Sister' this poem is in part concerned with Newbolt's sister Milly who had previously died in 1903. This is the 'dear dead name' of the penultimate line. Although outwardly a simple poem describing a walk with his daughter in the woods on a spring morning, the invocation of his sister suggests one of Newbolt's bigger and more perennial themes, notably the way in which the past continues to impact and resonate in the present.

The Presentation – Along with 'Amore Altiero' this poem saw Newbolt considering in a more philosophical way both love and his own personal relationships. They were singled out by Newbolt's Wiltshire neighbour and fellow poet and novelist Maurice Hewlett. In a letter to Newbolt he wrote, 'I was glad of your poetry book and grateful to you for sending it. You may rejoice, I believe, in "The Presentation" and "Amore Altiero." I rejoice in them and didn't write them! "The Presentation" is entirely beautiful, and I entirely agree with it. …' (Hewlett, 1926: 103).

Amore Altiero – The title translates as 'proud love'.

Against Oblivion – Although short, this exquisite lyric, which resembles some of the similar efforts of Yeats around the same time, touches again upon the theme previously addressed in 'Ave, Soror'. As the second stanza suggests, Newbolt had always been one to interrogate his own personal history.

Le Byron de nos Jours – The following lengthy explanation appeared at the end of the poem in its original publication:
The foregoing parody, which first appeared in *The Monthly Review* some years ago, was an attempt to sum up and commemorate a literary discussion of the day. On Saturday night, November 15, 1902, at the Working Men's College, Great Ormond Street, Sir Edward Clarke, K.C., delivered an address on "The Glory and Decay of English Literature in the Reign of Victoria." "Sir Edward Clarke, who mentioned incidentally that he lectured at the college forty years ago, said that there was a rise from the beginning of that reign to the period 1850-60, and that from the latter date there had been a very strange and lamentable decline to the end of the reign, would, he thought, be amply demonstrated. A glorious galaxy of talent adorned the years 1850-60. There were two great poets, two great novelists, and two great historians. The two great poets were Alfred Tennyson and Robert Browning. The first named would always stand at the head of the literature of the Victorian period. There was no poet in the whole course of our history whose works were more likely to live as a complete whole than he, and there was not a line which his friends would wish to

APPENDIX A

see blotted out. Robert Browning was a poet of strange inequality and of extraordinary and fantastic methods in his composition. However much one could enjoy some of his works, one could only hope that two-thirds of them would be as promptly as possible forgotten—not, however, from any moral objection to what he wrote. He was the Carlyle of poetry. By his Lives of Schiller and Sterling, Carlyle showed that he *could* write beautiful and pure English, but that he should descend to the style of some of his later works was a melancholy example of misdirected energy. . . . Charles Dickens was perhaps the most extraordinary genius of those who had endeavoured to deal with fiction as illustrative of the actual experiences of life. With Dickens there stood the great figure of Thackeray, who had left a great collection of books, very unequal in their quality, but containing amongst them some of the finest things ever written in the English tongue. The two great historians were Macaulay and Froude. To-day we had no great novelists. Would anyone suggest we had a poet? (Laughter.) After the year 1860 there were two great names in poetry—the two Rossettis. There had been no book produced in the last ten years which could compete with any one of the books produced from 1850 to 1860."

To this Mr. Edmund Gosse replied a week later at the Dinner of the Encyclopaedia Britannica. He reminded his audience that even the most perspicuous people in past times had made the grossest blunders when they judged their own age. Let them remember the insensibility of Montaigne to the merits of all his contemporaries. In the next age, and in their own country, Ben Jonson took occasion at the very moment when Shakespeare was producing his masterpieces, to lament the total decay of poetry in England. We could not see the trees for the wood behind them, but we ought to be confident they were growing all the time.

Mr. Gosse also wrote to the *Times* on behalf of "the Profession" of Letters, reminding Sir Edward of the names of Swinburne and William Morris, Hardy and Stevenson, Creighton and Gardiner, and asking what would be the feelings of the learned gentleman if Meredith or Leslie Stephen (of whose existence he was perhaps unaware) should put the question in public, "Would anyone suggest we have an Advocate?"

Sir Edward, in his rejoinder, had no difficulty in showing that Mr. Gosse's citation of Montaigne and Jonson was not verbally exact. Mr. Birrell added some comments which were distinguished by being printed in type of a markedly different size.

To the author of these lines, the controversy appears so typical and so likely to arise again, that he desires to record, in however slight a form, his recollection of it, and his own personal bias, which is in no degree lessened by reconsideration after ten years.

April on Waggon Hill – See 'Waggon Hill' above. As with other poems, Newbolt here suggests that the dead soldier both yearned for but is now reconciled with the landscapes of his youth. Brendon is a small village near the coast in the Exmoor National Park, close to the border with Somerset.

Songs of the Fleet – These six poems emerged as a consequence of Newbolt's week at sea as a guest of Admiral Sir Reginald Custance who had been Director of Naval Intelligence from 1899 to 1902. By May 1908 (the date of Newbolt's visit) he was in command of the Channel Fleet. Five of the poems were set to music by Charles Villiers Stanford and published as *Songs of the Fleet* in 1910. Given their premiere by the London Choral Society on 8 December 1910 they soon entered the repertoire. This was not the first time that Stanford had set Newbolt; *Songs of the Sea*, Op. 91(1904) featured renderings of 'Drake's Drum', 'Outward Bound', 'Homeward Bound', 'The Old Superb', and 'Waggon Hill' (under the title 'Devon, O Devon'). They were commissioned and sung by Harry Plunket Greene (see 'The Echo').

The War Films – The film in question is *The Battle of the Somme* (1916), a documentary and propaganda film shot by Arthur (Geoffrey) Herbert Malins in his capacity as an official cinematographer. It premiered in August 1916 and was seen by over twenty million people, although some viewers were upset by its vivid portrayal of violence. In a letter to Alice Hylton Newbolt wrote: 'What I wanted to tell you about was the Somme film. Of course it was bad, as they so often are, taken too fast, so that an ordinary march becomes double quick, and a running pace becomes a Walpugisnacht revel. But there are some fine moments in it … a purification of the emotion … the effect was to make me love them [the soldiers] passionately and to feel that the world would be well lost to die with them' (Newbolt, letter to Alice Hylton, 16 September 1916, quoted in Margaret Newbolt, 1942: 230–231).

St. George's Day – It was on St. George's Day that Newbolt's son Francis was wounded near Ypres: 'F. was knocked over by a bullet which hit his pack and got stuck in a cigarette case or some other metal box … Finally he was put to sleep by a shell, and doesn't seem to have known anything

APPENDIX A

till he reached the hospital ship forty-eight hours afterwards' (Newbolt, letter to Ella Coltman, 30 April 1915, quoted in Margaret Newbolt, 1942: 205). An awareness of this context adds to our appreciation of the poem as more than simply a piece of public propaganda.

Hic Jacet – The title translates as 'Here lies' and it is still used occasionally on gravestones. In this case it is clearly referring to the soldier who not only died fighting bravely but has passed on his beliefs and ideals to his son.

The King's Highway – Even as late as 1915 Newbolt was still committed to writing ballads. In a contemporaneous article in *The English Review* he spoke movingly of the ballad tradition, concluding that it was a form 'still of a very powerful enchantment, capable of moving the heart both with the sound of the trumpet and with the deeper music of the harp of Binnorie strung with remembrance of the dead' (Newbolt, 1915: 470). These sentiments, particularly what he perceived to be its memorable qualities, ensured that he continued with the form long after it was considered obsolete.

A Chanty of the Emden – The Battle of Cocos was a single-ship action that occurred on 9 November 1914 when the Australian light cruiser HMAS *Sydney* responded to an attack on a communications station at Direction Island by the German light cruiser SMS *Emden*. Of *Emden*'s crew, 134 were killed and 69 wounded, compared to only 4 killed and 16 wounded aboard *Sydney*.

The Toy Band – The poem is a retelling of the British Army's retreat from Mons (1914) in which Major General Sir Tom Bridges, the nephew of the poet Robert, used a tin whistle and child's drum purchased from a toy shop to rally two exhausted battalions on the verge of surrender to rejoin the British Expeditionary Force (BEF). It was published in *The Times* on 16 December and, as Newbolt revealed, was known to Prime Minister Asquith: 'The Prime Minister let out that he knew Tom Bridges, "He's one of the heroes of the war-there are three heroes- French and Haig, and Bridges." ... Then I told him the story of Bridges and the toy drum and penny whistles. He was enchanted with that, and Henry James more so' (Newbolt, letter to Alice Hylton, 9 December 1914, quoted in Margaret Newbolt, 1942: 195–196).

A Letter from the Front – Different in tone from anything Newbolt had previously written, this was a precursor of the freer form of writing that he sought to cultivate, not always successfully, in the following decade.

The Great Memory – History and the passing of time became of increasing concern for Newbolt both during and after the First World War. He was particularly interested in how cultural memory or 'Memory' could be preserved. In referring to an old acquaintance who had recently got back in touch Newbolt wrote that 'I can't bear to think that such characters fade and are forgotten: they must continue to shine in the Great Memory ...' (Newbolt, letter to Alice Hylton, 15 February 1915, quoted in Margaret Newbolt, 1942: 202).

A Letter to R.B. after a Visit – R.B. was Robert Bridges, whose 'new narrative method' (which Newbolt here attempts to imitate) was displayed initially in the dozen or so poems comprising *New Verse* (1925). Representing Bridges' contribution to nascent debates around free verse (a form he found constricting), and deriving from a detailed study and interpretation of Milton, his experimental lines thus had a definite number of syllables but an indeterminate number of accents and quantities. Bridges chose to make his line twelve syllables in length although they appear on the page as much longer, in the manner of free verse.

Cricket – Although Newbolt was a poor cricketer and sportsman he was nevertheless an enthusiastic player and had a lifelong love of the game.

APPENDIX B

GOODCHILD'S GARLAND: DIVERSIONS AND PERVERSIONS, 1909

The Joyous Ballad of the Parson and the Badger

NOT far from Guildford town there lies
   A house called Orange Grove,
And there his trade a Parson plies
   Whom all good people love.

> *Sing up, sing down, for Guildford town,*
>   *And sing for the Parson too!*
> *I'll wager a penny you'll never find any*
>   *That's more of a sportsman true.*

A neighbour came in haste one day
   With a piteous tale to tell,
But "A badger, a badger," was all he could say
   When they answered the front door bell.

> *Sing in, sing out, there's a badger about,*
>   *Send word to the County Police!*
> *He's playing the dickens with all the spring chickens,*
>   *And gobbling up the geese.*

Forth to the fray the Parson goes
   Beneath the midnight sky:
He threads the wood on the tip of his toes,
   And he climbs a fir-tree high.

PLAYING THE GAME

> *Sing never a word, it's quite absurd*
>   *To expect a badger to come*
> *And sit to be shot like a bottle or pot*
>   *To the sound of an idiot's hum!*

The clock has struck both twelve and one,
  His eyes are heavy as lead;
He heartily wishes the deed were done
  And himself at home in bed.

> *Sing ho! sing hey! the badger's away,*
>   *The Parson's up the tree!*
> *It's horribly damp and he's got the cramp,*
>   *And there's nothing at all to see.*

The clock struck two, and then half-past,
  The day began to break,
The badger came back to his earth at last
  And found out friend awake.

> *Sing boom and bang! the welkin rang,*
>   *The Parson "Hurrah!" he cried:*
> *The badger lay there with his legs in the air*
>   *And an ounce of shot inside.*

Happy at heart, though in pitiful plight,
  The victor crawled away;
He slept the sleep of the just all night
  And half of the following day.

> *Sing loud and strong, sing all day long,*
>   *Sing Yoicks! and Hullabaloo!*
> *But I've had enough of this doggerel stuff*
>   *And so, I think, have you!*

APPENDIX B

Nursery Numbers

I

LITTLE Boy Blue
Come blow up your horn!
Though if you do,
Little Boy Blue,
You'll probably rue
The day you were born.
Little Boy Blue
Come blow up your horn!

II

HOW doth the little busy bee
Improve each shining hour!
I chuckle softly when I see
How doth the little busy bee
Collect, not for herself, but me,
The sweets of every flower,
"How *doth* the little busy bee
Improve each shining hour!"

III

ONE a penny, two a penny,
Hot cross bun!
Did you say it isn't many—
One a penny, two a penny?—
If you did you shan't have any,
No, not one!
One a penny, two a penny,
Hot cross bun!

IV

THREE blind mice
See how they run!
Let me say it twice—
Three blind mice—
Nay! I'll say it thrice,
False alarms are fun—
Three blind mice!!!
See how they run!!!

Vice-Versa: Any Father to Any Daughter

IF butter-cups were white and pink
   And roses green and blue,
Then you instead of me could think
   And I instead of you.

Then I could daily give your doll
   Her early evening tub,
While you in easy-chairs could loll
   At some or other Club.

Then I could spell p-i-g pidge,
   And learn to sew like Nurse,
While you could take a hand at bridge
   And murmur "Zooks!" or worse.

Oh it would be as fresh a sight
   As ever yet was seen,
If butter-cups were pink and white
   And roses blue and green.

A Child's Philosophy

MOTHER, do you know I seem
Living always in a dream?
All the world is one big bed
Where we sleep till we are dead.

You and I and all the rest
Sleep near those we love the best.
Do not wake before me, Mother,
Let us wake with one another.

APPENDIX B

Up Early

WHEN I awoke the day was fine,
I could not stay indoors till nine;
So I got up and found my boots,
And started off to see the coots.

I crept the whole way down the stairs
As quiet as when I'm late for prayers;
I took a piece of school-room cake,
And ate it going towards the lake.

I saw a heron already there;
He never moved, but let me stare;
His legs were paddling in a pool,
He must have felt it nice and cool.

Then when I clapped I saw him go
With wings that seemed to meet below;
And when he sailed above the trees
He looked like something Japanese.

Sermon Time

THE roof is high above my head
   With arches cool and white;
The man is short, and hot, and red;
   It is a curious sight.

From the Dining Room Window

I AM not like
The greedy shrike,
I could not eat
A moth for meat;
I should not care
To scour the air
And swallow flies
Instead of pies.

But if I could
I'd be a mouse,
And in the wood
I'd make my house.
There I would feed
On nuts and things,
And sow the seed
Of fairy rings.

Evening Cloud-Land

THE sky is blue
   And like a sea,
Part of the view
   It seems to be,
Where harbours keep
   Their olden shapes
And islands sleep
   Between the capes.

APPENDIX B

Bed-Time

IT is not going to bed I hate,
   I'm not afraid of dreams,
But going before it's really late—
   How very hard it seems!

I do not mind in winter-time
   When all the world is black;
I lie and count, or say a rhyme,
   Till morning brings me back.

But now it makes me sad to think
   Of daylight going on,
And all the sky in rosy pink
   Long after I am gone.

To Diana

IN THE THIRD DAY OF HER AGE

OH! Diana, what is this that I am told?
It is said that you're already growing old!
   That your little scalp is innocent of hair as any minnow
   And your forehead seamed with furrow and with
     fold.

I'm afraid there must be truth in what they say—
I observed you couldn't walk the other day,
   And when scandalmongers ruthless
   Call you absolutely toothless
It is noticed that you cannot say them nay.

It's a pity, when one comes to think it o'er,
For you've yet to live some eighty years or more,
   And you'll cut a funny figure
   When you're seventeen times bigger
If you look like this when half a stone's your score.

Now you know as well as I do what I mean,
Though you chose to look so solemn and serene.
   I shall some day with my chaffing
   See your Majesty a-laughing,
And be paid for playing Jester to a Queen.

Aspirations of Age

A SIMPLE child, dear brother Jim,
   That lightly draws its breath—
Whether you call it "her" or "him"
   A simple child, dear brother Jim—
I'd be, if I might have my whim,
   Henceforward till my death,
A simple child, dear brother Jim,
   That lightly draws its breath.

A Christmas Carol

MOTHER has a horrid cold,
   Father has lumbago,
My sore throat is nine days old
   And will not yet away go.
I drink no drink but listerine,
   I eat no meat but sago,
But my head's as tight as a tambourine
   And my cough's a plague O
              Wuff, wuff, wuff,
My cough's a downright plague O.

A National Anthem

LET dogs delight to bark and bite
For 'tis their nature to.
At morning, evening, noon and night
Let dogs delight to bark and bite,
The true-born Britain loves a fight—
   Men best, but dogs will do.

      Chorus.
*Let dogs delight to bark and bite
   For 'tis their nature to.*

A Pig in the Making

THERE was a Pig
Who danced a jig
  Before his mother's sty.
She said "Go out
And use your snout,"
  But he replied "Not I!"

Now it is wrong
To go so long
  Without your proper food,
But wronger much
To answer such
  A kind Mama, so rude.

The Frugal Aunt

SHE dined upon a cold poached egg
      Saved from the breakfast table.
Contrast her lot with ours, I beg,
  She dined upon a cold poached egg:
    While we were munching mutton-leg
      As thick as we were able,
She dined upon a cold poached egg
  Saved from the breakfast table.

Rosy-Cheeks

A NYMPH who was named Rhodonopsis
  Had a habit of sleeping in copses,
    Which was hardly discreet
    In a lady so sweet,
For at last she was eaten by wopses.

At the Sea-Side

IT rains on the umbrellas here
    And on the ships at sea.
Whether the sky be close or clear
    It rains on the umbrellas here,
And if you stayed for half a year
    Your verdict still would be
It rains on the umbrellas here
    And on the ships at sea.

The Fairy Ship

    AS I went down through Eden Vale
        I saw a lovely sight,
I saw a ship of fairies sail
    Among the willows white.
The captain and his tiny crew
    They all were dressed in green,
And when the wind too gently blew
    They sang this song between—
O who will come to Fairyland, to Fairyland, to Fairyland,
O who will come to Fairyland and see the Fairy Queen?

    As I ran down through Eden Vale
        My heart was loud with joy,
I waved a bonnet like a flail
    And shouted "Ship ahoy!"
I'm sure they must have heard, at least,
    I thought they might have seen:
But always when my shouting ceased
    They sang their song between—
O who will come to Fairyland, to Fairyland, to Fairyland,
O who will come to Fairyland and see the Fairy Queen?

They sailed away through Eden Vale
    They left me there on land:
And oh! to think I could not hail
    A ship so near at hand!
Perhaps it was that what I heard
    The fairies did not mean,
But I remember, word for word,
    The song they sang between—
O who will come to Fairyland, to Fairyland, to Fairyland,
O who will come to Fairyland and see the Fairy Queen?

The Chamber of the West

THE Sun has gone to bed and drawn his curtain,
But he has not yet said "good-night," I'm certain,
Because between his shutters, where it's red,
I see the light burning by his bed.

Finis

NIGHT is come
    Owls are out,
Beetles hum
    Round about:

Children snore
    Safe in bed,
Nothing more
    Need be said.

Index

'Admiral Death' (Newbolt) 10, 128–129
Admirals All (collected works) 4, 9–11, 12, 14, 41, 129
'Admirals All' (Newbolt) 8–9, 125, 128
Africa, scramble for 12
'Against Oblivion' (Newbolt) 134
Aladore (Newbolt) 38, 130
'Almore Altiero' (Newbolt) 27, 134
American War of Independence 125
Amis, Kingsley 26
'April on Waggon Hill' (Newbolt) 25
 see also 'Waggon Hill'
Archer, William 9
Arnold, Matthew 43
Arnold, Thomas 18–19
Arthurian stories 15–16
Asquith, Prime Minister H.H. 137
Auden, W.H. 47
Austin, Alfred 11
'Ave, Soror' (Newbolt) 133–134

Baldwin, Prime Minister Stanley 44
ballad form 3, 4, 18, 30, 35, 130, 132, 137
'A Ballad of Sir Pertab Singh' (Newbolt) 36
The Battle of the Somme (film) 136
Belgium, invasion of 32
Bell, Vanessa 128
Benbow, Vice Admiral John 125

Betjeman, John 4, 36–37
Bilston, Staffordshire 4, 5
Binyon, Laurence 9, 34
 'The Burning of the Leaves' 49
Blake, General at Sea Robert 14, 16, 129
Blunden, Edmund 45
Boer War 9, 12–14, 17, 20–21, 24–25, 126, 128, 131–132
The Book of the Blue Sea (Newbolt) 33
The Book of Cupid (Newbolt and Alice Hylton) 28
The Book of the Grenvilles (Newbolt) 33
The Book of the Happy Warrior (Newbolt) 34
Booth, Imogen 130
Bower, Reverend Anthony 5
Bridges, Major General Sir Tom 35, 137
Bridges, Robert 9–10, 35, 45, 138
British Academy 30
British Empire 2, 13, 18, 21–22, 25, 49, 50
Brittain, Vera 39
Brooke, Rupert, 'Peace' 34
Brown, T.E. 6
Browning, Robert 132, 134–135
Buchan, John 44
Buchanan, Robert 9
Buller, Redvers 21

Burne-Jones, Edward 15
'Le Byron de Nos Jours' (Newbolt) 28, 134–135
Byron, Lord 125–126
Byron, Vice Admiral John 125

Campbell, 1st Baron John 8
Campbell, Roy 3
Campbell-Bannerman, Henry 21
Carlyle, Thomas 16, 135
'A Chanty of the Emden' (Newbolt) 35, 40, 137
children's literature 28, 33, 37, 42, 43
chivalry 3, 7, 15–17, 31, 35, 39, 41, 50, 130, 133
Christianity 12, 23–24, 38–39
Churchill, Winston 2
Clarke, Sir Edward 134–135
'Clifton Chapel' (Newbolt) 10, 17, 32, 130
Clifton College 5–6, 19, 22, 23, 39, 132
Coleridge, Mary 8
Collingwood, 1st Baron Vice Admiral Cuthbert 125, 133
Collins, William 130
Coltman, Ella 8, 28, 48, 137
commemoration 3, 20–30, 37, 41, 132
'Commemoration' (Newbolt) 22–24, 26, 132
Connolly, Cyril, 'Theory of Permanent Adolescence' 3
conversational approach 37, 45, 131
Coole Park 46
Corbett, Julian 42
Corpus Christi College 6–7, 31, 48
Cory, William Johnson 8, 127–128
cricket 5, 17–18, 138
Curzon, Viceroy of India Lord 127
Custance, Admiral Sir Reginald 31

Davidson, John, *New Ballads* 14
de la Mare, Walter 28, 32–33, 48–49

'The Death of Admiral Blake' (Newbolt) 10, 129
Dickens, Charles 135
Dixon, Richard Watson 10
Drake, Francis 14–15, 16, 131
'Drake's Drum' (Newbolt) 1, 9, 17, 50, 126, 136
Duckworth, Margaret 8

Eby, Cecil 34
'The Echo' (Newbolt) 130
educational reform 3, 42–44
Edwardian era 1, 18, 20–21, 49, 50
Effingham, 2nd Baron Charles (Howard of Effingham) 125
elegiac poems 3, 25, 37, 51
Eliot, T.S. 49
Elizabethan era 1, 14
Elkin Matthews' Shilling Garland 9–10
An English Anthology of Prose and Poetry (Newbolt) 44
Englishness 4, 11
'An Essay on Criticism' (Newbolt) 28–29
Essex, 2nd Earl Robert Devereux 125

A Fair Death (Newbolt) 7, 8–9
'Farewell'(Newbolt) 35
'Fidele's Grassy Tomb' (Newbolt) 29–30, 130
The Fighting Téméraire (Turner) 10, 126–127
film 38, 41, 136
First World War 24, 30–39, 40–41, 44–45, 51, 128, 137
free verse 138
French Revolutionary War 126
Froissart, Jean, *Chronicles* 15, 130
'From Generation to Generation' (Newbolt) 133
Fry, Roger 6
Fuller, Roy 49

INDEX

Furse, Ralph 37–38
Furse Jackson, Vanessa 4

gender roles 27–28
Georgian poets 30
Germany 9, 29, 30, 32, 34, 36, 47
Gladstone, Prime Minister William Ewart 130–131
Goodchild's Garland (Newbolt) 4–5, 28
Gosse, Edmund 135
Gray, Foreign Secretary Sir Edward 31
Gray, Thomas, 'Elegy' 23
'The Great Memory' (Newbolt) 138
Grecians group 8
Gregory, Lady Augusta 46
Grenfell, Julian 39, 40
Grenville, Sir Richard 125
Grey, Dorothy 30
Grey, Sir Edward 133

Haig, Field Marshal Douglas 6, 16, 31
Halbwachs, Maurice 46
Haldane, Secretary of State for War Richard 31
Hardy, Thomas 26, 135
 'Men who March Away' 34
Hawke, 1st Baron Edward 126
Hawke, Lord 10, 14, 16
Hayward, George W. 18, 127
'He Fell Among Thieves' (Newbolt) 17–19, 22–23, 127, 129
Henley, W.E. 11, 14, 49
heroism 3, 7, 11, 14, 16–17, 19, 21, 24, 34, 38–40, 49
'Hic Jacet' (Newbolt) 35, 137
Hodgkin, Dr. Thomas 133
Holmes, Edmond 32
'Homeward Bound' (Newbolt) 132, 136
Hope, Anthony 6

Housman, A.E. 25–26
 A Shropshire Lad 26
Hylton, Alice 28

'Imogen' (Newbolt) 130
imperialist principle 2, 10, 13, 17, 22
'The Invasion' (Newbolt) 36, 130
'Ionicus' (Newbolt) 8, 127–128
'Ireland, Ireland' (Newbolt) 2, 27, 130–131
The Island Race (Newbolt) 4, 10

Jonson, Ben 135

Keats, John 6
'The King's Highway' (Newbolt) 40, 137
Kipling, Rudyard 1, 11, 49
 Barrack-Room Ballads 25
 'For All We Have And Are' 32
 'The Islanders' 29
 'The Storm Cone' 47
 'White Man's Burden' 12
'Kruger Telegram' incident 9, 126

landscapes 3, 45
Lang, Andrew, *Longman's Magazine* 8
Lang, Archbishop of Canterbury Cosmo 6
law career 7
'A Letter from the Front' (Newbolt) 37
'A Letter to R.B. after a Visit' (Newbolt) 138
Liberal politics 2, 7, 8, 21, 25, 30, 33, 41, 44, 50
'The Linnet's Nest' (Newbolt) 45–46
Lloyd George, Prime Minister David 33
Low, Sidney 126
loyalty 30, 130
Lubbock, Percy 28

Lucretius, *De Rereum Natura* 19, 127
lyrics–ballad distinction 4
Lytton, 2nd Lord Victor Bulwer-Lytton 43

Maitland, Frederic William 128
Malins, Arthur (Geoffrey) Herbert 38, 136
Malory, Thomas, *Le Morte d'Arthur* 15
Masterman, C.F.G. 33
medieval themes 7, 15–16, 35
Medley, Rev. J.B. 29
HMS Menelaus 125–126
'Messmates' (Newbolt) 10, 129
'The Middle Watch' (Newbolt) 31
'Minora Sidera' (Newbolt) 16, 128
modernity 30, 40–41, 45, 49, 51
Monro, Harold 37
Montaigne, Michel D. 135
The Monthly Review 2–3, 21, 134
'Moonset' (Newbolt) 131
Mordred (Newbolt) 8, 16
Morris, William 135
Murray, John 3

Napoleonic Wars 125, 126
nationalist sentiment 2, 9, 11–12, 34
nautical/naval themes 4, 10, 27, 33, 36
Neill, A.S. 43
Nelson, Lord Horatio 14, 16, 21, 125, 126
Nemo, Henry (Newbolt's pseudonym) 4–5, 28
Netherhampton, Wiltshire 38, 45, 48
'new narrative method' 138
New Paths on Helicon (Newbolt) 3, 44
Newbolt, Celia 30
Newbolt, Francis 37–38, 136–137
Newbolt, Henry
  autobiography 5, 7–8, 30, 131
  death 48
  early life 5–20
  later life 40–47
Newbolt, Margaret 28, 48, 128
Newbolt, Milly 133
'Newbolt Report' 42–43
'The Nightjar' (Newbolt) 46
Nine Years' War 125
Noble, Sir Andrew 133
'The Non-Combatant' (Newbolt) 129
'Northumberland' (Newbolt) 133
Noyes, Alfred 28

The Old Country (Newbolt) 130
'The Only Son' (Newbolt) 26, 132
Orchardleigh Park 8, 18, 28–29, 45, 48, 130, 131
'Outward Bound' (Newbolt) 132, 136
Owen, Wilfred 39, 40
'Oxbridge' education 127
Oxford, Corpus Christi College 6–7, 31, 48

Pack, Sir Denis 128
Palmer, Herbert 129
Parker, Captain Peter 125–126
pastoralism 26
patriotism 3–20, 22–23, 25, 33–34, 40–41, 50, 129, 132
Pease, Howard 133
Peppin, Arthur 130
Percival, Bishop John 6, 39, 132
Percy family 133
A Perpetual Memory (collected works) 4, 45, 47
'A Perpetual Memory' (Newbolt) 39
Phillips, Stephen 10
Picton, Sir Thomas 128
Plato 6
Plunket Greene, Harry 130, 136
Poems New and Old (Newbolt) 4, 36, 44
political engagement 2–3, 6, 12, 22, 27, 31, 47

INDEX

Pound, Ezra 3
Pre-Raphaelites 15
'The Presentation' (Newbolt) 27, 134
propaganda 38, 136, 137
public schools 3, 6, 15, 17–19, 22–24, 32, 34, 40
Pudney, John 49

Quiller-Couch, Arthur 6

'Rilloby-Rill' (Newbolt) 28
Rodney, 1st Baron George Brydges 125
Romanticism 43, 46
Rose, H.J. 19
Rossetti, Dante Gabriel 15
Rousseau, Jean-Jacques, *Emile* 43

Sackville-West, Vita 128
'Sacrementum Supremum' (Newbolt) 133
sacrifice 20–22, 38–39, 41
The Sailing of the Long-Ships (collected works) 4, 20
'The Sailing of the Long-Ships' (Newbolt) 131
St. George's Day (collected works) 4, 41
'St. George's Day' (Newbolt) 136–137
'San Stefano' (Newbolt) 9, 125–126
Sassoon, Siegfried 39
satire 28
'The School at War' (Newbolt) 22, 132
'The Schoolfellow' (Newbolt) 132
Scruton, Roger 2
Second World War 49
'The Service' (Newbolt) 36, 41
Seven Years' War 125, 126
Shakespeare, William 135
  Cymbeline 130
Shaw-Stewart, Patrick, 'Achilles in the Trench' 34–35

Sidgwick, Adam 6
Sitwell, Edith 3
Songs of the Fleet (collected works) 136
'Songs of the Fleet' (Newbolt) 31
Songs of Memory and Hope (Newbolt) 4, 20, 27–28
Songs of the Sea (Newbolt) 136
'A Sower' (Newbolt) 26
sport–warfare connection 17
Stanford, Charles Villiers 136
stanza structures 18
'The Star in the West' (Newbolt) 47
Stephen, Leslie 16, 128, 135
Stevenson, Robert Louis 135
Strang, William 128
Submarine and Anti-Submarine (Newbolt) 33
Swinburne, Algernon Charles 135
'Transvaal' 14
Symbolism 14, 15
Symons, Arthur, *Amoris Victima* 14

Taken from the Enemy (Newbolt) 7
Taylor, Samuel 8
HMS *Temeraire* 126–127
Tennyson, Alfred 6, 15–16, 134–135
Thackeray, William Makepeace 135
Thomas, Dylan, 'If I Were Tickled by the Rub of Love' 26–27
Thompson, Francis, *New Poems* 14
Threlfall, Will 39
The Tide of Time in English Poetry (Newbolt) 44
'The Toy Band' (Newbolt) 35, 40, 137
Turner, J.M.W. 10, 127
The Twymans (Newbolt) 5

Victorian era 15, 20–21, 50, 134
Victorian sentiments 1, 11, 18, 21, 40, 51
'The Vigil' (Newbolt) 12, 36, 40, 128

'The Viking's Song' (Newbolt) 26
'Vitaï Lampada' (Newbolt) 1–2, 17, 19, 23, 40, 127
'The Volunteer' (Newbolt) 13, 131–132

'Waggon Hill' (Newbolt) 131, 136
'The War Films' (Newbolt) 38–39, 41, 136
War of the Spanish Succession 125
warfare–sport connection 17
Watson, William 28
   The Purple East 12

'When I Remember' (Newbolt) 133
Wilde, Oscar 14
'Wonder and Reason' (Newbolt) 46–47
Woods, Margaret 10
Woolf, Virginia 128
working classes 7, 25, 29

'Yattendon' (Newbolt) 133
Yeats, William Butler 33, 46
Younghusband, Francis 6